Filter of Time

One Woman's World

Carol L. Shafer

Cover: Anders C. Shafer

ARC Press of Cane Hill
P.O. Box 188
13581 Tyree Mountain Road
Cane Hill, Arkansas 72717
501-824-3821

Printed in the United States of America

Dedication

*To Boyd C. Shafer,
my life-partner
of sixty years*

Table of Contents

Foreword

These stories and sketches came
out of dreams, problems, concerns, or
illuminating moments that have been
part of me at different times in my life.
Some are clearly autobiographical, others
only obliquely so; all are mixtures of
events and people, real or imagined, from
my journey. Written over a period of
thirty years they are offered here
unrevised.

Much as a painter gathers together
a selection of paintings for a
Retrospective Show and then stands
back a little amazed at the total effect, so
I look at these and discern a great variety
of odds and ends that have structured
my life.

I present them here for I believe that
a past remembered is not enough; it is
only useful if it nourishes the renewal.

¥

The Wind is Always Blowing on the Prairie

Anna still lives. Long after she is gone and I am gone and the prairie is cemented over with highways and people live in high-rise apartments above the earth or in deep tunnels below --- the wind will continue to blow on the prairie and people will have even more need of the courage and love of which her life speaks.

The Wind is Always
Blowing on the Prairie

Whenever I think of Anna I feel a stirring in the air and hold my head as she does, as if facing a strong wind. Anna lives alone in a little house in a prairie village. She is no longer young but her days are full. If she reads this she will be surprised to learn what unexpected and long-forgotten parts and pieces of her are now a part of me. I give them to you, for who among us does not need to stiffen his back once more?

Anna is a distant cousin of my father. She came to our house from the country when I was five, working for her board and room while attending our Academy. Her father, Jorgen Petersen, had been reluctant to let her go. She could cultivate a row of corn as clean as a man and shuck it as fast as her brothers. Hurdling a gate like a boy she would say she was going to grow up and be a "lady". Big Pete pondered his daughter's ambition for a whole season and finally deemed it proper that one of his girls go away for an education. And that was how Anna came into my life.

If the Nike of Samothrace had been found on a Viking ship she would surely have been modeled from Anna's ancestor. We children were vaguely aware that Anna's hair was silken yellow, that her eyes were china blue and her mouth a sensitive tremble, but we knew well that the swift movements of her shoulders and her long sure limbs set up new vibrations in our house as elusive as the whispering of corn fields or the twittering of a barn swallow.

My first actual memory of Anna is of her
voice, soft, fast, a little surprised. One hot June
night she was bathing my brother, sister and me
in the dormitory bathroom for our family lived
in the empty Academy during the summer. I got
out of the tub and peered into a long dark hall
toward a door at the far end which opened to a
brilliant sunset sky. Anna shook the towels at
us.

"Run, you little squeakers, run hard."

We ran, arms and legs free. At the far door
we stared at the golden sky with its silhouettes
of factory chimneys and roof tops. Then we
raced back to the young voice that chuckled,
"Run hard." Running absolutely free was pure
joy.

Anna's bedtime stories were animated
narratives of the farm. "True stories," we would
beg. We shivered when she told how her family
ran for the cyclone cave just as a twister lifted
the chicken house and pigpen and deposited
them across the road, leaving the house intact.
We were terrified by her tale of the bull that
killed her Uncle Robert and the boar that ate
fingers off little children. We loved the ghost
story of the white horse that always appeared in
the pasture before thunderstorms. Our favorite
was Anna's bareback ride on the runaway.

"One night last summer," she would
begin, "Clara and Dagmar and I went down to
the creek in the lower pasture to swim. No, no
bathing suits. The work horses, very tired after
a long day in the fields, were there having a
drink. Clara, always up to mischief, dared me to
ride Ted bareback. Ted was the oldest of Paw's
horses. He was brown and wide as a door. Paw

started out farming with him and Bess. I walked up to him natural-like, talking all the time. 'Whoa boy. Whoa there, that's a fine horse.' I patted his neck, then grabbed hard on his black, sticky mane. The next second I was up on his back. Ted just stood there, petrified like, too scared to move (I was dripping wet, you know.)

"Then with a high neigh like this," and she would illustrate, to our great delight, "he pawed up the bank of the creek and began to run. He put his head down, he shook, he jumped, he even kicked. All this was way out of his line. The other horses stared at him; they couldn't believe he would do such a thing. Then they began to jump and kick, too. First thing you know, we were all racing around that pasture a million miles an hour. All I could do was hang on for dear life and pray nobody would drive by on the road and see me.

"Paw was up at the house, smoking his pipe on the back stoop. He heard the commotion, took his shotgun from the entry and hurried out. About that time Ted decided to gallop into the barn and I, wet hair flopping up and down and, believe me, scared to death, stuck on. Ted ran right into his stanchion and I slid off. I yelled to Paw I would never do it again. Clara brought me my clothes."

More fun than running free in the corridors would be to ride a runaway horse. How thrilled we children were. Scared to death, she said, but she hung on.

Anna was not with us long before another story, one our parents did not know, was added to her repertoire. Students were ordered never to walk through the cemetery at night, but Anna came through often as a shortcut. One night a man followed her.

"Faster and faster I walked," she said as we sat breathless on our bed. "He kept on coming just as fast. I turned to the left to wind around a grave, he turned to the right and took the opposite path. Where the paths come together I was just three steps ahead. Around the graves we went, the little dark trees weren't big enough to hide behind and the marble markers just stood in the way. We got close to the iron gate and I could see it was shut tight. It's high on each side and low in the middle, so I made a run for it -- sailed over it like a deer -- and was out on Eastern Avenue with street lights and the streetcar line. Yes, I looked back just once. He was climbing over the gate, clumsy as any city dude. I was almost home."

How many times in my dreams have I run this race; how many times have I sailed over the cemetery gate, the pursuer close behind; how many times have I looked back just once to see his defeat!

The time came when Anna's bravery was put to test. Papa himself told us after Big Pete had given him the details when he brought Anna back to school after summer vacation. It happened in the evening, chore time on the farm. Anna's brother Carl and the hired man were leading the new Holstein bull, named Oscar Reynolds III, from the barn to an outside pen. The animal broke away and bunted Carl who fell face down in the yard. The beast backed away, pawing the dirt. The hired man shouted and tried to drag Carl away but the bull rushed him and caught him on the shoulder. Anna,

gathering eggs in the barn, heard the shouts
and reached the yard just as the crazed animal
tossed the hired man in the air. Remembering
that her father had once quelled an enraged bull
by threatening his sensitive nose with a pitch-
fork, she grabbed a long-handled fork from the
barn and advanced.

"Oscar, go!" she shouted. Holding the
shining fork in front of her she walked steadily
toward the bull. Oscar lowered his head and
blew through his nostrils, but his rolling eyes
caught a glint of the sharp tines and he hesitated. Anna then backed toward the corral and
he came snorting but not risking attack. A few
steps and they were both in the enclosure. Anna
reached the far side of the pen before he rushed.
The wooden fence was too tall to vault, still she
pulled herself to the top before he struck. The
force of the brute against the boards threw her
far on the other side. Her head struck the
cement watering trough as she fell.

By this time Big Pete and the others were
there and the gate to the corral was swung shut.
Carl was not badly hurt, the hired man got a
very bad shoulder out of it. Anna regained consciousness with a great buzzing in her head.
She never was able to hear much with her left
ear again.

"Wild bulls," said Papa to us, "are not
exactly predictable. The risks of courage are
great. The price may be demanded the rest of
one's life."

One Fourth of July our family was invited
to a Lutheran Church picnic on our uncle's
farm. Such special occasions live forever for
children who are lucky enough to be given

them. Cousins and friends were there, the Petersens among them. Long tables on sawhorses were set up in the grove, their tablecloths anchored against the wind by casseroles of fried chicken, dishpans of potato salad and centerpieces of layer cakes and apple pies. Firecrackers popped off at forbidden times and places, even when the minister stood up on a chair to say the blessing.

In the afternoon we children played pompom-pull-away and nine-step on the front lawn while the young men and women gathered for athletic events -- Indian wrestling, races in gunnysacks, weight lifting and stunts. A blond man who won many events was John Nelsen, my uncle's new hired man just over from Denmark. I saw Anna and went to sit beside her on a wagon tongue. She straightened my hair ribbon for me. She did not clap for John Nelsen but smiled at him whenever he looked her way, which was often.

In the evening the young people danced circle dances in the hayloft and Anna and John were often partners. All that stamping and laughing seemed a strange way for grownups to act and we children ran outside and lay in the cool grass waiting for the fireworks.

Finally the fireworks came: Roman candles, sparkling fountains, the skyrocket that fell too soon and burned a hole in someone's car top, the rocket that went off backwards and caused the menfolk to talk a long time before lighting more, then the final successful skyrockets that rose like shooting stars as great sighs of admiration went with them. At last the real stars of the sky took over and children were gathered into cars and buggies to be taken home. In the lane our car lights shone on Anna and John Nelsen walking hand in hand.

Mother said to my father in the front seat, `"I see Anna has a beau."

"Anna has a beau, Anna has a beau!" I repeated in singsong to my brother and sister and we giggled.

"What noise is that?" said Papa. "Anna deserves a good man. They make a fine pair. There will be no more snickering in the back seat."

The War came. Grownups talked about President Wilson, Foch, Hindenberg.

"Yes, it is farther away than across Lake Michigan," my father explained. "Across the ocean men are fighting and dying."

John Nelsen enlisted. Before he left he and Anna were married. During the winter he was sent over there.

"Over there, over there," we children sang. "And we won't come back till it's over over there."

In the fall, almost my birthday, Anna's son was born. Mother took me to the country to see the new baby.

"So tiny," she said to Anna.

"A little Johnny," Anna said, "if he does not come back."

Anna was different, quieter, not at all ready for a lark. She stood very straight and dignified on the porch as she waved us goodbye.

"Is Anna grown up now?" I asked. Mother nodded.

On Armistice Day we walked in parades and beat drums. The War was over over there.

Cornhusking time came and went and snow fell on the Petersen farm, but Anna and little Johnny still waited for soldier Nelsen to come back. One afternoon when I came home from school Anna was at the door. There was no need to ask, her face was glowing, John had returned.

"Last Saturday!" she said.

Mother poured coffee but Anna only sipped hers. "I was sitting in the dining room nursing Johnny, you know, the bay window where Mother keeps her plants. No word from John except a letter after the armistice saying he was still alive. I thought maybe he went back to Denmark. What if he had lost an arm or a leg! He was so proud of his fine body. If he couldn't work he might not want to come back. I prayed hard. It was not too much to ask, was it?

"I looked up into the buffet mirror and saw a man in a soldier's uniform standing in the door behind me. His face was so tired, so thin, his eyes so bright blue. We stared and stared. He walked in, all the time smiling at me in the mirror!"

She cried; Mother cried; they both patted me and shook away their tears. "We'll stay with Paw until spring," Anna said, "then work the Andersen farm beginning March. John is home!"

Mother held me in her lap after Anna went even though I was a big girl now. I asked her why grownups cry when they are happy. "Being really happy is so wonderful it hurts," she said.

Anna and John worked the Andersen farm for three years and then rented the Vestergaard place on shares. Steadily their

livestock, poultry and family increased. Anna's
chicken money met their grocery bills, her
garden yielded a winter's supply of vegetables.
Rows of home-canned corn, plum and strawberry preserves, pickles, applesauce filled her
fruit cellar. She drove the cream to town and
helped with the milking. A sister for Johnny,
Dagmar, was born then a husky boy they
named Peter, and finally a girl they named after
me.

On Johnny's tenth birthday our family
was invited to dinner. Going to the farm was still
a treat to us children, even though I was now a
high school senior. I expected to be in college
soon -- all this "family stuff" would give way to
bigger things.

We turned into the tree-lined lane leading
to a square white house and Johnny, who had
been waiting for us, proudly opened the gate.
Racing down the lane came Dagmar and little
Peter and a shaggy collie. They jumped on the
running boards and jigged up and down hilari-
ously, as if riding horses. The collie barked and
kept an anxious eye on them. Anna waved her
apron to us from the back porch.

"Welcome," she said in her quiet voice,
and we knew we were truly welcome. "John is
finishing chores in the barn."

Papa and the others went to the barn
while Mother and I stood a minute with Anna on
her steps. The sun was dropping like a giant
pumpkin behind a hazy Indian summer horizon.
Fall chrysanthemums bloomed yellow and
bronze under the kitchen windows. The air held
a tang of wood smoke and fall.

"Anna, you didn't tell me," said Mother,

noticing Anna's pregnant figure. "Are you strong enough, so soon?"

Anna smiled, shook her silken hair out of her eyes and looked toward the barn. The wind had died down and in the evening stillness all sounds came to us magnified -- the high voices of the children, the clang of milk pails, the mewing of cats waiting for warm milk to be poured into their special saucers, the whispering conversation of hens settling themselves on their roosts for the night.

"I will manage," Anna said, turning to go in. "Life -- it is good."

The dinner table was covered with a white cloth. When we were seated John sat proudly at the head looking over a platter of golden fried chicken, Anna at the other end with the baby in a high chair beside her. John said a blessing in Danish and the children mumbled "Amen". We ate with enthusiasm. Papa complimented Anna rather formally and she blushed as she rose to replenish the bowls of whipped potatoes, the creamed gravy, and the crab-apple pickles. There was talking and laughter but when Johnny interrupted the elders to tell about his pet pig he was hushed very sharply by his father. How we all exclaimed when Anna brought in the candlelit birthday cake. Yes, I thought, what Anna said was right. For the Nelsens and for us too -- life is surely good.

I finished college and took a job in Chicago. My parents moved to another city. One day Mother wrote me about visiting John Nelsen in the state hospital near them. Troubled with ulcers of the stomach since the War, he had lived his own way, trying to ignore his condition. Now he could eat nothing. The doctors feared he was too weak for an operation. Mother telephoned Anna to come.

A week later I received more news. "Your father and I have been visiting John every evening. You remember how jolly he always was. He joked about his stomach, said if he could have some of Anna's cooking he'd be ready in two days to do the harvest. In fact, he didn't want Anna to come at first, there are seven children and two hired men for her to care for. Clara drove her down Friday. They left at three in the morning, hurriedly, coming in housedresses and sweaters. Anna seems more hard of hearing. She could not believe John's condition serious. She sat with him all day Saturday but got restless. She said if they drove all night they'd make the farm by breakfast.

" 'Stay another day,' John said, 'What is one more day in a whole lifetime?' So she stayed. Sunday afternoon as she sat beside him he reached for her hand and stared at her hard, saying nothing. He kept on looking and looking at her with his intense blue eyes. All of a sudden she realized he was gone. He had looked back to her as long as he could, to the furthest edge of the divide.

"Papa is helping with arrangements. Anna seems lost, she agrees with every plan, smiles in a twisted way. 'John says for me to stay on the farm,' she repeats. I don't think she hears much of what we say, maybe just as well. Her love was great while it lasted. I think it will carry her through."

One fall several years later I revisited the community where I had lived as a child and I stayed with my aunt. We drove out into the country to see Anna. I had forgotten how much sky there is on the prairie, how deep and black the soil, how the cornstalks rattle as they complain of the breeze, how the fat lazy cattle look up so nonchalantly from their grazing in the oat stubble, and how pungent are the smells of growing things, ripening drying things, even stinky things.

Over all moved the wind, the ceaseless prairie wind. How could I forget it? "It's always blowing," Mother used to say fretfully. "Why complain?" Papa would reply. "It's a part of the human condition we can do nothing about, only accept it."

As we topped a rise in the road Auntie pointed. "That's Anna's place, the old Petersen homestead. Yonder, see that mound, that's what is left of the sod hut Big Pete built when he first came to this country in the '70's. As soon as he could, he built this house. Fifty years ago it was one of the finest homes around. Dear me, look at it now! Big Pete moved on when Anna was a little girl, but now she is starting all over again on the same homestead."

By a mailbox marked "John Nelsen" we turned in. The barn needed paint but its ridge-pole was straight and hay bulged from the loft. The granary stood empty, one wall collapsed like a folded venetian blind. An ancient hayrack and a new red seeder sat in its runway. Fat white chickens walked importantly in and out of the doors of a shiny yellow chicken house. The old farmhouse, protected from the north by two rows of pines and cottonwoods, sat quietly on the rise, battered, nondescript, smoke coming

from the chimney of the kitchen ell. A brown
dog got up stiffly on the porch and barked
inquiringly as we stopped at the house gate.

Anna appeared, untying a blue apron as
she hurried out to unlatch the gate. At first she
did not recognize me, then her face lighted and
she extended both hands in welcome. I feared to
look at her closely, knowing she must be
changed. Her blonde hair was cut and hung
straight as a child's and blew around her face in
light threads. A loose checked dress draped her
firm body like a toga. She was straighter than I
remembered. I met her eyes and saw that she
smiled only with her mouth, her eyes no longer
crinkled at the corners.

She led us through the kitchen which
smelled of milk pails and baking bread into a
formal parlor where we sat stiffly. A rug, three
rockers, an old victrola furnished the room --
strangely bare. She asked about my family.

"And you?" I asked in turn. "Tell me so I
can take word to my parents."

"It's quite a story," she said, folding and
unfolding her apron across her lap. "After John
died I tried to keep up the farm, but couldn't.
Paw let us move into his tenant house rent free.
With the veteran's pension we managed somehow, but seven children wear out a lot of shoes.
Of course, we weren't building anything for
tomorrow. John would say it wasn't good.

"Last March this place was for rent and I
wanted to take it. Paw was agin it. Johnny and I
talked and talked. Johnny is sixteen now, wish
you could see him. Well, Paw finally was per-
suaded and said he'd help us with three cows. I
had my chickens yet, about 300.

"It snowed hard the day we moved. Paw and the boys brought over two wagon loads -- beds, range, rugs, some food. It was so cold they decided to bring the rest of the stuff the next day. So Johnny and I built a big fire in the cellar laundry stove of the old place to keep my canned goods from freezing and we came on here. I put the kids to bed and sat in the kitchen with my feet in the oven to keep them warm and went over the whole thing again. What if the crops failed? What if the cows died? Maybe Johnny should go to college and not be a farmer. If we lost, we lost everything but the pension. The new place, now that we were in it, needed more repairs than we realized. Plaster was down, windows rattled like guns, the porches had no steps, even the pump handle was broken. Besides, it seemed spooky being in the house where I was born and where Grandma died. I was ready to bundle the whole raft of kids back into the car and make for home. The telephone began ringing the party line; I thought it peculiar so late at night. Harry Jackson was saying Paw's tenant house was on fire -- come quick, bring pails. Our old house!

"Yes, everything went. They saved the barns, though. But my picture of John, my piano, my canned fruit, my best dishes. The laundry stove, I guess. It was just like a funeral. We cried, even Paw. When Johnny and I came back the next morning the sun was coming up behind this place and it looked mighty good, I'll tell you. 'We can't go back now, Maw,' Johnny said. It was decided. John would have said God Himself had a hand in it."

"And now?" I asked.

"We manage. No steps on the front porch yet," she laughed. "I have a hired man in heavy times. The garden was good. Let me give you a basket of eggs to take back."

In the kitchen Anna took her bread from the oven and rubbed butter over the crusts. The last pan contained a Danish coffee cake. We sat at the kitchen table while she made coffee and cut the spicy cake. A pile of mending filled a chair by the window. A gasoline lamp sat on the table. A barrel of cobs stood behind the kitchen range. On a bench near the door was a wash basin and a water pail with a dipper.

"We have no fancy things," and she chuckled a little as she poured the coffee. "But we have all we need to be strong and warm. Hard work, of course, but so is anything worth while."

She said goodbye at the gate and pointed proudly toward the schoolhouse on the distant hill. Black dots of youngsters were on their way home. A flash of dinner pails in the slanting sun signaled to Anna that her children saw her. She waved to us all the way down the lane.

If Anna reads this she will smile, maybe even chuckle. "So she remembered all that!" She will step to her front door, open it to the restless prairie breeze, and stand a long, long time re-membering -- remembering not only the things I have told you but amazing things I never will know. The wind will blow her hair from her eyes. She will straighten up and welcome it now as an old friend.

Easter Sunday Morning

This glimpse of my family I reread with sadness as half of the members of the group are now gone. But the circle of love remains and although stretched to cover children and their children it has never broken, not once.

Easter Sunday Morning

It was Easter morning, an hour before sunrise. I dressed quickly in warm ski pants and mackinaw and slipped into the upstairs hall, careful not to awaken the rest of the family. But Papa had heard me and came to his door as I reached the turn on the stair landing. I waved goodbye to him and he nodded at me as I disappeared down the steps on my way to the sunrise service. I can hear the click of the rug guards on the stairs as I tip-toed down, hear the slow metallic tick of the mantel clock in the living room, see the sudden brightness of the white tablecloth on the big round table in the dining room when I switched on the hall light and the shine on Mother's cups in the circular china closet. I can smell the rubbers in the front entry as I sat on the hall-tree seat and hunted for my galoshes. Through the curtain on the front door I could see a street light still on and a gray, cold morning outside.

This was Easter of the year I was seventeen. This was like all the Easters I had known - church, Easter eggs, family reunion - a day of celebration and renewal. An ordinary Easter. However, I was a senior in high school and this Easter never did come again, never again for me and never for my family as the circle was broken when I went away to college. This day has never come for my children either, much as I might wish to hand it to them, a gift of perfect security and basic order, a universe with plan and a family of unshakable, unquestioning affection and understanding. A day so rare that even the wish to return promises more pain than pleasure, and the door dare not be thrown open full.

We met that morning at Wilma's house. Five of us had planned to hike to the sunrise service at the Country Club, two miles or so across the railroad bridge and over the golf course to the highest hill. The idea had seemed an exciting one on Wednesday night when we sat with ice cream sundaes in the candy kitchen after our weekly basketball practice. Dorothy had giggled and said she'd never be able to get up so early. Wilma had offered to phone her in time. Ruth, who lived in the country, had been doubtful; but the Silly Six (our special club) would stick together as they always did. It was a vote. So Wilma was dressed and waiting when I got there. Her serious face was flushed and she was worried that the moist air might spoil her voice for the cantata solo in church later. Her blonde hair, often stringy, was pinned into close waves and her nose was shiny, but her million-dollar figure could never be hidden even in hiking clothes. Dorothy came next, awake, but not much more, her coat wide open and her scarf trailing, her brown eyes amused as usual. She was always the first to laugh, and even after an early marriage and five boys her letters were full of giggles. Ruth did not come after all; her father would have had to drive her into town. But Helen and Gertrude arrived just as we had decided to go without them; Helen, crisp, efficient and matter-of-fact, who became the schoolteacher and then the wife of a rich rancher; and Gertrude with Madonna-black hair and Irish blue eyes, already the prototype of the society matron she became.

Exactly what we said or did I cannot be sure. I recall the dangerous hurry over the railroad trestle, the puffing and chatter as we stumbled through the paths along the river, the shivering huddle together as we stood among many others waiting for the sun to come over the ridge of the golf course. I recall the hush before the singing, and then the singing. But only Wilma's voice comes clear -- she, my best friend, with a golden tone that was an unmistakable gift, a gift she generously returned all her life to the little town in which we lived. No bird song comes clearer to me than hers, flying strong and free over those morning hills that Easter morning as the first rays of brilliance slashed the sky.

Together we tramped back to town. The zest was now gone; whose idea had this been in the first place, how silly can a Silly Six get? Dullness clamped over us until we at last reached home. Mother had suggested we breakfast together at our house, so I had planned it, food, timing, all the details. The clumsy big stucco house that was home seemed like a castle in the wilderness when we finally reached it. There was the smell of cocoa as I opened the door to usher in the gang -- warm, rich, relaxing cocoa, and there was Mother in a frothy apron coming into the hall to greet us.

There was, of course, a pile of Easter eggs in a basket in the center of the table and there was laughter and the sound of chairs being pulled up as we all sat down. Papa had waited to eat with us. My brother, fifteen, ignored us, preferring to read the funny paper. My two sisters, younger, joined us, too. I recall the familiar

brief pause, as Papa cleared his throat and
looked around the table before we all bowed our
heads for grace. On Easter it would be a special
grace. Papa's words were usually the same as he
always used but they never sounded the same
because he talked directly to God. Although he
addressed God at all times with the utmost
respect and humility there was also the
undeniable fact that Papa was a man in God's
image and had every right, even duty, to speak
about anything that was pending or of immedi-
ate concern to him and his family. And so, as
Papa requested, God came down and blessed
each and every one of us that moment in
memory of His Son who rose from the tomb of
darkness into eternal life.

Mother brought in the turkey platter full
of bacon and scrambled eggs and I carried in
rows of toasted cinnamon rolls on Mother's
Royal Doulton serving dish. The number of eggs
eaten on Easter morning was always a matter of
competition. My brother not being at the table to
win such a contest, Helen probably ate the most
that day. She, who had the tiniest waist, always
surprised us at picnics and fish fries with her
magnificent appetite.

Church was at eleven. I had to be there
early because I sang in the choir. Mother was
always the one to hurry us in preparation.
Someone's shoes always needed shining. The
ironing board would have to be put up in the
cold back summer kitchen in order to press
Papa's pants, for some reason always neglected
on Saturday. I don't remember dressing that
Sunday, but I know I had a new hat. I probably
had my clothes carefully laid out on the bed in

my room. My room, a room of my own at the head of the stairs! It was large and opened onto an upstairs porch. Ah, Juliet! No, the porch railing was wide and heavy, forbidding, from below. But such privacy! On a summer night, with the door wide open and the white curtains pulled back, the moon poured down upon it as lovely as in any place before or since, and its soft mystery held, as it has for all young girls, the burden of my dreams.

There was a crowd at the side entrance to the church that morning. The Sunday School rooms had been opened to provide seating for the overflow. I stood on the bottom step waiting for a path through to the choir room. My new pink straw hat was stiff. I had never had a wide brim before. It tilted too far forward whenever I looked down, so I had to stand perfectly erect and in spite of myself look ladylike. The two beautiful Granston sisters, just home from college, stood near me. They wore fur pieces and flowered hats and were surrounded with perfume, a perfume so wonderful I knew it cost much more than Evening in Paris. I followed Mr. Stone's eyes as he too, standing below me, appreciated their elegance and beauty. Mr. Stone was our recreation director, a blonde well-muscled young man who supervised swimming and basketball for the church young people and who was absolutely impervious to the adoration of every member of the Silly Six. Dorothy would "pooh, pooh!" but the rest of us were all agreed that Mr. Stone was about the most ideal man we had ever seen.

At that moment Mr. Stone looked at me. He started to greet me with the genial cordiality that he always gave his teenage crowd, a greeting that always put us in our place, right at his feet. But something startled him. Was it my new hat? I flushed at his amazed stare. Papa, too, had remarked about my hat when he saw it, "Well, who is this young lady?" Mother had said, "It is about time." Brother had kidded me about the sails. Now Mr. Stone apparently didn't like it. But at least it had made him look, I consoled myself. And he did look. It was with new appraisal. For the first time a grown man looked at me as a woman. Not long, he caught himself, and smiled before he turned away. I went on into church a bit unsure and uneasy and took off my hat as soon as I reached the choir room.

There was a more-than-usual bustle in the choir room: Mrs. Groves breathlessly explaining why she was late; Mr. Bemis handing out the music and telling us how to arrange the pieces in proper order; someone's robe losing a clasp; men in the bass section clearing their throats and singing "me, me, mo, mo"; Mrs. Jackson, our director, reassigning places to fill last-minute absences. On Easter she was nervous, more than ever, in spite of wearing her diamond earrings and a rose corsage given her by her husband. The last minute she would instruct us, "now in the cantata, remember to go in gently on the hosannas, especially you men. Begin low and *soto voce*, so we can really build it up." How I loved that build-up! "Hosanna, hosanna in the highest! Hosanna to our King!" My hair at the nape of my neck tingled even in practice when we came in full force, the pipe organ too, in a tremendous glorious smash of sound.

The organ was beginning, we could feel it
throbbing on the heavy low notes as we filed in
and self-consciously took our choir seats. Easter
Sunday was indeed very special. Flowers everywhere, the minister in a new black suit, people
filling every pew as well as chairs in the aisles,
the ushers wearing white boutonniers, the
children clean and well-behaved, sitting beside
their parents, the radiant sun in its first burst
of spring warmth pouring through the colored
window of Christ at Gethsemane. Joy was in the
air. And suspense. We knew the story, yet
waited to hear it told again. All week we had
suffered with Jesus and on Friday gone to
church under darkened skies to remember how
He had cried out on the cross, "Father, hast
thou forsaken me?" and finally, "Not my will, but
Thine, be done." And when Mary came to the
sepulchre at sunrise on Sunday morning,
behold, he was not there. An angel sat upon the
stone which had been rolled back from the grave
and said, "Fear not ye.....He is not here: for He
is risen, as He said."

And so we all exulted, the great hymn at
the end, "All hail the power of Jesus' name, let
angels prostrate fall. Bring forth the royal
diadem and crown Him Lord of all -- and crown
Him Lord of all." The organ roared and filled the
farthest room with quivering sound, the voices
rose together in praise. I looked down and saw
Papa and Mother with little sister between them,
and brother and sister on each side, standing in
the pews at my left. The minister held up his
arms in benediction, and once again the Lord
who had suffered for us all arose from the grave
and walked among us. Darkness may be ahead,

evil may try to win, but we all stood together, family, church, friends, to celebrate the fact that this wonderful world of ours would be redeemed, as surely as spring follows winter and as certain as the love of parents doth endure.

That was Easter when I was seventeen.

Three Scholars

This account of a weekend at Buzzard's Bay is part of a chapter in an unpublished novel concerned with the struggles of a graduate student and his wife. He is attending a university in New York. The time is the mid-30's. The three scholars, on various steps of the academic ladder, would not be greatly different today. Some of their attitudes would have changed but the steps on the ladder remain. And knowledge itself, the goal of the scholar, has become far more than a measure of professional attainment; today it holds a life-line for human survival.

Three Scholars
From Chapter XXII
Bend Down the Bough
(an unpublished novel)

Part C

"Time to get up, lazybones." Laurel stood by the bedside with a cup of coffee in one hand. "Smell."

Paul opened his eyes a mere slit and groaned. She leaned over gingerly in order not to spill the coffee, and placed a small kiss on his forehead.

"I'm awake." He sat up very touseled. Laurel set the coffee cup on a little table just out of reach.

"What's the idea?"

"I know you're always groggy when you sleep in the afternoon." She brought him his bathrobe. "Get on your feet and you'll be all right."

"Groggy? Hell, I'm in good humor. I don't give a damn about anything. Come and kiss me again, and not a peck either."

"Your coffee is getting cold."

Shivering, Paul got slowly out of bed, giving the bed canopy a mean look on the way. "Speak to you of love, all I get is 'your coffee is getting cold.' It is cold in here. Shall I build a fire?"

"They expect us downstairs, I guess."

He sipped the coffee. "Ah, that's better.

How long did I sleep? Four-thirty now! What's going on downstairs?"

"Not much. Just comfortable things. I helped Sarah with the dishes and we put a ham in the oven. A tremendous thing, a whole ham. You can smell it when you go out in the hall."

"Suits me." He pulled Laurel down beside him on the sofa. "And the others, what are they doing?"

"Let me see. Dr. Adams was in the living room reading when I came up. Dr. Baker and Mrs. Adams played cribbage after lunch. Do you know how? I don't either. A little while ago Mrs. Adams (they all call her Merrie) played some Grieg and Chopin and a little Gershwin on the piano. You'd have liked it -- the afternoon light -- the fire -- the delicate music. The notes of the music seemed to reach out and weave us all together into a beautiful special world."

"Why do you always look so serious when you try to be lyrical?" Paul touched her cheek.

"Don't make fun of me. It *is* hard to describe feelings. I wish you would tell me something. What is it that makes music so satisfying? Maybe while we create it or just listen to it we become for that duration a piece of some kind of perfection."

"Of course, darling." He kissed her beneath her ear. "System, plan, order. Man is constantly in search of it. What else did you do?"

"Oh, the best thing of all I forgot to tell you. There are violets blooming right out in the grass, hundreds of them. Remember, fifty cents for a spindly little bunch in the subway at Times Square? Well, I just raced around picking them like crazy. Mrs. Baker said, 'The older one grows the more important spring becomes.' Here is a violet in my buttonhole. Oh, it's withered!"

She laid the limp flower on Paul's knee. He inspected it closely and handed it back. "What else did you women discuss?"

"Oh, nothing important, just enjoyed ourselves poking around in the leaves looking for new plants coming up. I talked about the settlement house. Mrs. Adams told about the Lunts in the opening of the *Sea Gull*. Lynn Fontanne can create an entire mood with a single gesture, like hitching up her skirt when she stands. I wish we could go to see them."

"Why not, when we are ready to celebrate, and you know when that will be."

"Paul, I've decided something."

"Hmn, what?"

"Well, it's more of a hunch than a decision." She lifted the violet and spun it round and round. "Much as I admire Mrs. Adams and much as I know you admire Dr. Adams, still I think when I get along in years I will try to be more like Mrs. Baker. In the first place, Mrs. Adams has so many talents I don't have. She seems so restless, so much in a hurry, so . . . "

"Well, after all, four children . . ."

"I know. I can't seem to put my finger on it, but Mrs. Baker always seems to understand. She's been through all this and requires no explanations. She isn't forcing me to take sides. I feel comfortable and accepted, and then I feel stronger. Don't you?"

Paul studied a moment. "Yes, you may be right, but as to the men, I would stand behind both of them. They are simply at different stages in their lives. Adams is in there pitching, in the thick of his research and teaching, the most productive time of his life. With power and reputation established he's in the control seat. Maybe still on his way up the ladder. Now, on the other hand, Baker, John Charles Baker, is what he will always be. There is a completeness about him. We can stand off and look at him whole. This could still be a fruitful time for him too, even though he is retired. I hadn't thought it through before. Now he can really speak his mind, his reputation is made and he can't be fired. If he is wise this is the payoff. He can come closer to the truth than ever before.

"I suppose to see him keeping on like this should give us courage. Work is what gives meaning to his life. History, the search for understanding, needs the work of much more than one lifetime. My God, I ought to have the guts to finish my thesis, to make it damn good, too."

He stood up. "Go on down. It's five o'clock. I'll be right with you."

Part D

The dinner was over. Sarah had filled all the coffee cups a second time.

"Mrs. Baker," said Professor Adams, pushing back his chair and breathing an obvious sigh of contentment, "this was a feast I shall long remember. Superb ham! You don't cure your own, by any chance?"

"No," Mrs. Baker smiled. "Sarah's husband smoked this one for us. I'm glad you like it for you'll have more of it tomorrow for breakfast. This is actually our Easter dinner a day in advance, in your honor." Turning to Mrs. Adams she went on, "How much fun if you had brought the children. We'd have hidden Easter eggs in the garden."

"The children would have loved it, but I'm not so sure about the garden," said Mrs. Adams, reaching for a cigarette from a silver dish. In a turquoise velvet blouse and a wide black ribbon banding her bright hair, she lent elegance to the table.

Laurel studied Mrs. Adams' face and decided that her beauty resided not in her features, regular enough, but in her vivacity and sparkle. In a mirror above the buffet Laurel could see half of her own face reflected beside Paul's back, so rigid and proper from the rear. Moving slightly she saw her full reflection -- pale, remote, and indefinite. Her hair, however, burned dull red in the candlelight and the yellow chiffon scarf, knotted carefully around her neck, flared up like a spring jonquil. Yellow seems too bright, almost raw. Much better in this setting is Mrs. Baker's dress, an old-fashioned lace the color of dusty garnets. The bosom of the dress was filled in with a flesh-colored net which rose to a high collar. Black ribbon on the edge of the collar set off Mrs. Baker's finely lined face like a Sargent portrait. Laurel visualized Mrs. Baker in that dress pre-

siding at past dinner parties and receptions.
How proud she is of Dr. Baker and of her family!
Through them she lives in her totality, but
through each of them individually she is also
vulnerable. Her hand shakes as she holds her
coffee cup. Yet actually she had unpredictable
and compounded strength.

Mrs. Adams was talking about her housekeeper. "Bojenka has been decorating Easter
eggs for a week. The Easter bunny will arrive
without fail on Morningside Drive."

"He's coming to the Dean Street Settlement House, too," Laurel said. "I've never seen
such elaborate eggs as those decorated by a
Ukranian couple in the neighborhood. Their
eggs are blessed by a priest and exchanged with
friends and kept for years."

"A charming idea," Mrs. Baker remarked.
"I should like to visit the settlement house, but
we seldom come in to New York any more. I
would enjoy the Easter music. What is the Philharmonic playing tomorrow, Merrie? We'll have
it by radio."

"*Parsifal*, with Bonelli and Gordon and a
choir. There's also a matinee at the Met with
Melchior and Flagstad. But I find *Parsifal*
heavy."

"We'll have it on the car radio on the way
back tomorrow," Dr. Adams grinned. "We can
turn it off if it gets too much."

Laurel thought something should be said
about Easter, the real thing -- not just eggs and
music. "To be out in the country in the spring,
at Easter, is wonderful," she started, feeling her

way. Everyone listened politely. "I'm so happy we came. To see and feel the new life growing -- the hope -- the new always coming from the old -- the faith that is resurrected each year. That, to me, is Easter. The resurrection is probably the highest point in most religions, don't you think? That is after all what gives man hope."

"Absolutely," Mrs. Baker smiled and nodded at Laurel, then nodded her head several times as if repeating it to herself.

Mrs. Adams exchanged an enigmatic glance with her husband and took up her cup for a last sip. No one took up the topic and Laurel realized she had spoken out with more emotion and earnestness than she had planned. She retreated immediately. Her cheeks flamed and she felt like a child that should have stayed upstairs. *I probably seem naive, or worse than that, platitudinous. But just the same, I believe what I said, and it is true, about hope.* she thought.

Filling his pipe, Dr. Adams turned to Laurel and began a discourse on comparative religions. The discourse developed into a description of spring festivals. Soon everyone had a word to say. Dr. Baker said spring reminded him of fishing and that reminded him of some muskie pictures in his study he wanted to show them. He leaned on the arm of his tall grandson, Lee, as they made their way down the hall to the study.

Laurel and the men followed into a small book-lined room. Every chair seemed to be covered with magazines and books. On one

side of the flat-top desk was a pile of folders;
spread out were sheets of paper covered with
neat, fine writing. The professor picked up one
of the sheets, glanced at it as if he were going to
read from it, then set it down on top of the pile.

"Last draft, I hope, " he said. Then pulling
out some envelopes from a file, "Let me see,
'Summer of 1930,' no, 'Christmas 1928,' no --
ah, here -- 'Summer 1936.' "

Paul stood beside the folders on the desk.
He was not interested in pictures of fish, not
even of John Charles Baker and fish. "Chapter
VII" was written on the folder that topped the
pile.

"You have reached the final draft of your
book, sir?" Paul asked. Surely Dr. Baker
couldn't be serious about the photos; he was
only trying to be kind to Laurel.

"Yes, Paul, I hope it's the final one. But
come, look at this muskie, twenty-five pounds! A
giant! We were floating down the Flambeau, one
day of vacation left, no muskie -- just a few pike.
I had on a long sucker as bait, tossed it out, and
-- wham -- this fellow took it. He put up a terrific fight; I'll never forget the sight of his great tail
flapping as he dove under. Elizabeth was
actually frightened when she saw him. Louie
gaffed him when I got him up along the boat."

"Magnificent!" Laurel said. "I've never
caught one that large. You look mighty proud."

"Naturally." Dr. Baker adjusted his glasses
for another look. "Of the few achievements in my
life this ranks high, a twenty-five pound muskie!
Paul, you ought to take up fishing. You can

handle a boat."

Putting his hand on Paul's shoulder, Dr. Adams remarked, "He's a fisher of men."

"Whether they want to be caught or not," Paul snorted.

"Teaching is like that," said the old professor, shaking his head.

Lee, who had been sorting through the pictures, looked up. "Old Bailey didn't even realize he was in danger this morning."

"Few do," said Dr. Adams, packing the tobacco down hard in the bowl of his pipe. "They're punch-drunk with some moonshine -- power, money, fame what-have-you."

"But we couldn't let him drown. We had a human obligation to pull him in." Paul half questioned as he held a match for the professor's pipe.

Dr. Adams took a few draws until his pipe was well lit and then waved it at his host, "What is your opinion, Dr. Baker? Is it our duty to rescue poor ignoramuses who don't give a damn?"

The elderly man took the question seriously. He walked around his desk and fingered the paper upon which he had been working. "Duty? Perhaps. Obligation, I like better. But it's hard to assign roles. We are all in this together, the human race -- for the last 10,000 or 500,000 years, for the next 10,000,000 for all I know. Only little by little do we build, little by little, little by little." He lifted one sheet of paper covered with his neat script and let if fall. It slid off the desk and Lee picked it up quickly.

"Sometimes it is the poor ignoramuses that perform the rescue, unknowingly maybe, but they perform. Today, Paul and Lee, the rest of us stood by to aid. Tomorrow someone else. But we keep on. The human race keeps on. The more we understand of the dangers the more obligation we feel. On the other hand, the greater the vision the more discouraged we often become, we see so little accomplished in one lifetime."

He placed his hand affectionately on the arm of his tall grandson. Lee put his own hand over it and gave his grandfather an open boyish grin.

"You, Lee, are just starting." He gripped the arm hard. "Youth, youth, tremendous possibilities. The big chance, the unknown discovery lies ahead." He began to walk nervously around his desk and stopped at the window to stare out. "Then before one realizes it, middle-age arrives. Sadness comes. Most of the dreams will never be accomplished, the 'big chance' never came. Yet there is a strength at that time, a new strength that comes with realization. A more attainable goal is set, some things have proven worthwhile, for a few things one can fight."

Turning from the window he looked at each of them. He seemed to shrink as he approached his next point. He lifted his hands, thin, veins bulging, spotted with blotches, looked at them abstractly and dropped them at his side. "And then -- one day we are old. There is no gamble left. We stand revealed, to ourselves and to the world. There is little more one can do with the time left." His eyes fell upon his manuscript and his back straightened. "But I have discovered each age has its compensations. Youth has dreams and energy, middle-age has power, but there comes a time of freedom, freedom from the urgencies of self. I know myself and how I stand; now I can forget myself and look at the world with clearer eyes."

Laurel took an impulsive step toward him. He smiled at her. "And what I see, young lady, still looks good!"

Appearing in the doorway, Mrs. Baker suggested that they all listen to a new record, a Mozart symphony done by the London Philharmonic. They settled themselves in the living room as Lee put on the first record. Paul lounged in a wing chair by the fire with Laurel on a footstool beside him. Dr. and Mrs. Adams chose the prim love seat, Mrs. Adams kicking off her shoes and tucking her feet under her skirt. Mrs. Baker took a low rocker and Lee sat on the floor by the phonograph, on hand to jump up and turn the records. The elder professor tried two chairs and finally stretched out full length on the window seat. Laurel wondered if he were dozing. When the symphony ended he sat up quickly, shaking his head and ready to talk.

For a while the talk was about music. Mrs. Baker said it would never be like the old days when Toscanini conducted, although Barbirolli and Koussevitzky were fine. Merrie Adams offered to get Mr. Baker tickets for Marian Anderson's final concert on the eighth of May when he said he would be in the city. Lee turned in a news broadcast, keeping it very low.

Dr. Adams walked over to lean closer and listen. "Might as well see what has happened in the world while we are out here enjoying it."

"Any new developments in Spain?" asked Dr. Baker, putting another log on the fire.

"Loyalists' forces cut in two by Franco," reported Lee.

"Better news from China," Dr. Adams said. "Japan has suffered its first major defeat. Suchow is the objective now of a smashing counter-offensive."

"What about home?" asked Mrs. Baker. "At least we have no war."

Assuming a weather reporter's voice, Professor Adams answered, "Weather tomorrow will be fickle, sad for Easter hats. Eighty-one degrees in New York Friday, cooler today. Who can say about tomorrow?"

"Francis, you're making fun of me. I'm no longer fascinated with temperature readings. I'd be more interested in the state of the nation."

"Well, Mrs. Baker, that too is fickle. Business index is at a new low, 78.2 I believe. In President Roosevelt's Thursday Fireside Chat he outlined a program of spending designed to break the back of the recession. Five billion was asked. Some say pump-priming won't help. The problem is to get production started again."

Mrs. Baker held up her hands. "Enough. The budget problems of my family are enough for me. The national budget!"

"I heard that Fireside Chat," said Dr. Baker, leaning one arm against the mantel.

"That man has a way with him; he's convincing. Yet I couldn't help wondering if he were neglecting some other programs that might have made this sort of emergency spending unnecessary. A good administrator catches the emergency before it comes to a head. But that is difficult, requires a long time in control and a long-time view. Jefferson saw that problem when he was president -- used the embargo to circumvent catastrophe. But it didn't really work. By the way, Paul, your thesis on Jefferson, what are you trying to do?"

Paul walked over to the fire. "An analysis chiefly. Using the Louisiana purchase as a case in point, I'm attempting to show Jefferson's philosophy at work."

The old man nodded. "An analysis, difficult for a beginner. Yet I'm glad it will be more than an exercise in fact-gathering. We've got to train for more than that. Need perspective to see the minutiae within the flow of time."

"Do you mean, sir, to see the event or fact as nearly as possible in terms of its own day, to place it as honestly as possible in its niche?"

"That and more." The old man teetered back and forth on the balls of his feet. "You, as a writer of history, have to see the event before and after; see it in motion."

"To see after an event implies a certain value judgment, doesn't it, Professor? That puts us on dangerous ground," said Dr. Adams as he too came over to the fire. "Of course, without knowing what comes before an event we cannot understand it, and without knowing what comes after the event we do not know its relative importance in the narrative that follows."

Paul frowned and ran his fingers through his hair.

"I don't pretend to have all the facts, he said, "though I've gone through stacks and stacks of documents. In trying to show ideas as well as events in motion I have to evaluate, to judge them in the light of Jefferson's total accomplishments. Perhaps I should have stuck to a straight monograph."

The elder professor spoke quickly.

"Don't give out now. Francis thinks you will make it. He's a first-rate teacher, if I do say it." The old man laughed.

"If you want to know it, young man, I was *his* teacher. You are in the enviable position of being ahead of both of us. Let me show you what I mean."

He hurried out of the room and returned quickly with his arms full of books which he stacked one on top of the other before the fireplace. They made a little tower in front of Paul.

"There they are. Twelve volumes, my total contribution to the history of man. This is the first one -- on the Constitution. Here is the one that gave me a black eye among my colleagues; amusing how it is now considered a standard reference book for undergraduates. This little one took the most out of me, the philosophers of the 18th century, actually not in my field but perhaps my most inspired piece. Well now, Paul, when your thesis is done you can place it on top of this pile and go on from there. That's what I mean by being ahead of us."

Paul looked at the irregular tower of books, realizing they contained the whole of the great man's thought. He dared not, even in imagination, place his little book on top of them.

"I see, I see what you mean." Paul stumbled slightly. "Of course, even though I have your twelve volumes for support there is no guarantee that I'll reach as high a point of wisdom as have you, Professor Baker. There is also this problem -- can I go right on from there? Didn't I hear you say, just today, 'each generation writes its own history in answer to its own special questions' ?"

"You should have been a lawyer, quoting me back to your advantage." the aged man looked quite young in his face as he put one hand on top of his books and leaned forward. "Let me say it this way: life -- human life on this planet -- seems to be becoming more complex, opportunities for better or for worse are increasing at a rapid (almost geometric) rate. Just so will history, *his story*, have to become, in each succeeding decade, wider, deeper, more all-embracing. 'Reason is itself a growth,' they say. You are right, Paul, to say history is not the description of one layer of time on top of another layer, put down like geological deposits, until we arrive at now, the top layer. Rather it is a process, an expansion, an ever-widening circle."

He flung out his arms, embracing them all and all of time as far as mind could penetrate. "I suppose when you come right down to it, Paul, your philosophy of history is really your philosophy of life. It has to be."

"And *your* philosophy of history, Dr. Baker?" Francis Adams asked pointedly. "Won't you fill it in for us?"

The old man pulled out a straight chair and sat down on the edge of it. "All right, you asked for it. But first, sit down and be comfortable. This will be more than one sentence. My philosophy of history: -- well, it goes something like this: In the growth process of life on this earth everything is organic. Civilizations, likewise, retain something of the old even though they are often formed in opposition to the old. A son develops many years in opposition to his father, yet in the end he becomes like him, with something new added. Look at our civilization -- we have Greek thought, Roman organization and law, Christianity, the scientific method. All these retained in spite of periods of opposition. Our present belief in individual freedom has been growing since the French revolution, even before. The promise of rational thought and the miracles of science were ushered in in the 18th century. On the horizon -- we see it especially in Europe today -- is the power of the collective state. It may be the pendulum swinging, it may be a new synthesis, who can tell?"

"Do you follow Hegel -- thesis, anti-thesis, synthesis?" asked Paul.

"No, the historical process is neither as definite nor as inevitable. I see it more as an ever-expanding flow with many circles, crossing and recrossing. And I may sound old-fashioned to you, and I suppose I really am." He reached

over and took his wife's hand and inspected it
as he talked. "But when all is said and said
again, I still believe in progress. I believe mankind is moving steadily, slowly, upward and
outward. We can go faster now, we control more
of the environment than before. No other species
of life has done that. Who knows to what
heights we may attain! It scares you when you
know the power we have."

No one spoke for a moment. Laurel visualized man's struggle upward and outward and
excitedly saw him flying off mountaintops,
shooting up in a great burst of fireworks, into
infinity.

"You encourage us with your faith." Dr.
Adams cleared his throat. "I wish I too could call
what we are doing progress, but I'm not as certain about our direction. Perhaps I'm more of a
relativist. I see history as a series of syntheses
that are always in the process of coagulating or
dissolving. Who can see the end? Complexity,
yes; solutions, no. And what about chance -- the
shape of Cleopatra's nose? Wasn't there a cup of
water that changed the course of a nation?"

"I don't believe it." The old man was
emphatic. "Chance, yes. But only for the
individual, not in the long haul. If there hadn't
been a Napoleon there would have been another
military leader. The broad outlines would have
been the same, maybe a century later or so. But
what is a hundred years more or less?"

"It's all I've got," Mrs. Baker remarked
laughingly.

"You are a special case, " the professor

teased. Then he went on seriously, "Too many people see only the tiny veins in the leaf, only the remote detail. But if one studies he can follow the veins to the stem, the stem to the twig, the twig to the branch, and finally the whole tree. The historian sees the whole tree. Some men, men of stature for the human race, not only see the tree but, if great enough, can take it up and shake it." He clenched his fist and shook it at them furiously. Passion reddened his face.

After a long tense moment Mrs. Adams pulled her feet out from under her skirts, stood up stiffly. "Well, if historians can see the whole tree, why don't more of them shake it? Bend its boughs just a little and help us. Mold the forces and show us how to avoid the mistakes of the past. Probably the historian doesn't believe what he sees. Maybe he doesn't care -- just plays a game of intellectual hide-and-go-seek. Unless you really change human behavior, where is the progress?"

"Mrs. Adams, we do change behavior," said Paul. "Without understanding, who can make intelligent choices? We wouldn't be teachers if we didn't believe that."

"I'll never be a teacher," Lee remarked casually from the floor. "I'm not easy with people -- they're too unpredictable. I'm going to take up chemistry, or math, get my hands on somethng concrete."

"Just like your father," Mrs. Baker said affectionately. "But Lee, even the physical sciences have their intangibles. You'll soon discover that. To me history has always been fascinating because it is life, life as it is lived and not artificially bottled up in a test tube. Now Francis, I know what you are going to point out. That history is life bottled up in books. But I believe we learn the most from history. As for the arts, they are wonderful, yet frankly they often bore me. They are so overwhelmingly ego-tistical. *Self*-expression can be very trivial."

"Don't be rough on the artist," Merrie Adams said, walking over to look at a water-color above the phonograph. "We are only trying to make a little isolated island of order out of chaos, out of life as it is lived."

"Remember, my dear," Dr. Baker reached again for his wife's hand, "the historian is an artist when he tries to write down the vision of life he sees."

The fire had burned down. One log flamed up very brightly with a sputtering fizz. The people in the room watched it until it died down and became red embers with the others. No one broke the silence. Finally Mrs. Baker stirred in her rocker.

"Does anyone want a cup of cocoa before we go up?"

"This is perfect, just this," said Laurel. It did seem perfect to her. The whole day had been a day of revelation. The evening had bonded them into a unity that would never disappear, even should they never sit together again. And tomorrow is Easter, a day of hope, of faith reborn. We are waiting at the door of the tomb, waiting for the stone to be rolled back. The new day is being born. We are all here: the ancient sage, the ones who are strong and proven, the ones who are beginning. *But why am I here? Why do they accept me and why do I feel at home? I have little knowledge. I have no talent.* And then she knew and her heart warmed to the glow of the brightest coal in the fire. She joined the circle. She belonged by faith. Perhaps she too would help roll back the stone.

Impressions

  During the war we (my Second Lieuten-ant husband, our two babies and I) were stationed for a time at Ellington Field in Houston, Texas. I was asked to write a description of life on our Housing Project for <u>Wingtips,</u> the area's mimeographed weekly. I sat down one morning before the children awoke and jotted this off. Even now I hear the planes droning and feel again the tightness and desperation of those dark war years.

Impressions
(from *Wingtips*, March 28, 1944)

The day begins before sun-up for those who live at Sam Houston Gardens. An alarm clock rings, a baby cries, a newsboy whistles. I glance out of my front window and see other similar front windows lighted up and down the avenue. I glance out of my kitchen window as I light the gas for coffee and see my neighbor tie her housecoat about her and reach for her coffee pot. Her kitchen shelves have gay paper edges. Maybe mine will too after I've been here as long as she.

Cars honk. Men step out of doorways to take their rides to the field. Doors slam. Porch lights are snapped off. A transport zooms up from the airport like a flushed bird and the air begins its throbbing. Dawn comes, more often gray than rosy fingered. Women sit quietly for a moment over a second cup of coffee before waking the youngsters for school.

Morning belongs to the domestic. I lean on my open door and inquire of the weather man, "Shall I wash today?" Water is soft and lathers are thick. A neighbor in slacks is shining her windows. Another is airing a mattress. Someone bangs a dustmop. As the sun comes out the clothes lines bloom. Little boys on tricycles ride fearlessly in the quiet road. A baby in a blue sweater sits in his play-pen and sucks his thumb and looks wide-eyed at Texas. A young bride walks past with grocery bags in each arm. Milk trucks and laundry trucks make their regular progress through the streets and the familiar maintenance truck dashes hurriedly to meet a call.

The day drones as do the planes overhead. Noon-time, sun-time, nap-time. Babies are taken to the clinic in the fine new community house. "Come again next month," says the nurse. "If we are still here," the mother answers.

"I followed my man all last year," said the nurse, "and I wish I could now." The baby cries loudly as the needle enters his arm.

"Oh Doctor, can't we immunize them against war too!"

The top of the day is the cocktail hour and the cocktail is Daddy. A sudden activity seizes the community. Cars with uniformed men go by. Boys shout and play machine gun. Little girls walk in the road with arms around each other. Women in fresh dresses and flowers in their hair sit on doorsteps holding babies. They wait for the right car to stop. Tantalizing smells of dinner are in the air -- steak, onions, gingerbread, hot biscuits, coffee. The airplanes circle above. Sometimes they trail white vapor as they fly toward the sunset. "Come in now," the mother calls, "Daddy is home and hungry."

In the gentle evening light men puff their pipes and stroll outdoors. They rub a spot here and there on a car and give the tires a speculative kick. In the springtime they take up a hoe and dig somewhere. If the neighbor is digging too, out come matches and cigarettes and the pause that refreshes. Radios sound, a typewriter clicks, planes keep on buzzing, children shout to one another as they run to make the goal.

Before I go to bed I take a quick walk. The moon is bright on the quiet street. Red and green lights of planes are now circling among the stars. The lights of the houses are going out early for the men have a hard day ahead. I see a mother lifting a child into his bed; I see four people leaning over a bridge table; I see a Victorian what-not on a wall; I see, in the next house, a model airplane and a camp chair in a bare room.

I turn into my own walk. "This is *our* house," my two-year-old daughter had said. A shadow falls across the door step. I will not look at it. It could be the shadow of a broken wing or even a ship's prow. Today this is our house and it is truly our home. Tomorrow - let us skip tomorrow and think rather of the day after tomorrow. Meanwhile I will pick the rose that someone planted at my doorway on Ratama Avenue in the Sam Houston Gardens, Federal Housing Project No. 41031.

Reconversion

This piece came at the end of the war. We lived in Washington, my husband in G-2 at the Pentagon. We and all our neighbors were sick of migrating and were hoping to find a home of our own someday again.

Reconversion
Or
Nothing Behind Me

I had tied on John's bib and was reaching for the soup ladle when the bread man tooted his horn in the court below.

"B'ed man," said John, standing up in his high chair.

"Bread man," said Ann, jumping off her seat. "I want to go down with you, Mummie." Four-year-old Ann was already General of the Household.

"All right," I promised. "You carry the money and I'll carry John. If we wait to help John walk down three flights of stairs the bread man will be gone."

On the first floor we met Mrs. Ray coming out of her door. She wore a blue chenille house-coat and was wiping cold cream off her face.

"He always comes at the wrong time," she sputtered. "Yet I suppose we can be thankful for him way out here in Arlington so far from the stores."

I nodded in agreement, set John down on his own tireless legs, removed from Ann's fist some orange peelings picked up on the stairway, and hurried out to buy a loaf of bread.

Several women were already in line behind the bread truck. The sun was hot in the courtyard. There was red brick to the north, east, south and west, up and down and all around, the battlements of war housing. One woman was joshing the bread man about the high price of the bread and pumpkin she had purchased. It was Mrs. Lane, who lived in our apartment building. Slow-gaited and heavy, she had long since found it convenient to forget her appearance. Her daytime garb was a pair of blue slacks and a wrinkled white shirt, her dinner dress -- the same. Her husband was an officer in the Navy and she had lived "around". Gradually she had discarded all but the "essentials," the essentials of an effortless existence. She gave the pie to her four-year-old son to carry up and yelled after him, "Watch out. If you squash it I'll whip you."

When it was Mrs. Ray's turn she bought three loaves of bread and some rolls.

"My three boys have terrible appetites," she explained. She was such a quiet hen-like woman. I often wondered what a red coat would do for her. One day I saw her wearing one and I lost faith in red.

Mrs. Harrison, who lived on the second floor in our building, was just ahead of me. Round and neat and bubbling, she was as usual breathless from chasing her household routine around the clock. She bought bread and a half-a-dozen doughnuts and then darted out to divert Butchie, her youngest, from the newly tarred roadway.

"Good to see you back, Mrs. Harrison," I said. "What luck house hunting in Albany?"

"Oh, haven't you heard?" She stopped to beam at me. "I thought you might have, it's all

I talk about. We've bought a house!"

Mrs. Ray turned back from the front step, the sun glistening on the cold cream on her face. "What's this I hear! The Major Harrisons have bought a house?"

"Go on," Mrs. Harrison waved her hand. "Cut the 'Major' stuff. We're almost out of the Army. It'll be 'Mister' from now on. Mister Harrison, if you please. Just another day to go. Yes, Butchie, you can have a doughnut, but stop your yelling." She shrugged her shoulders. "Almost lunch time, too, but what can you do?"

"Did you say you bought a house? What's that?" asked Mrs. Lane as she lowered herself to the entrance step and groped in her slack's pockets for a cigarette.

"Yes, a house, all ours." Mrs. Harrison's words came fast. "It's seven years old but in perfect condition. Far better than the war-built houses; the windows all fit; the doors work; the paint is still good. And too --- it is a thousand dollars less than most of the newer ones. We looked at everything for four days and on the fifth we found this. Just what we wanted!"

I stayed to hear more and let Ann and John play in the loose dirt beside the walk.

"Three rooms up and four down. Just right for us. A big living room way across the end of it." And Mrs. Harrison's arm swept a wide space in front of us. "And girls, a real open fireplace!"

"Ah, a fireplace. A REAL one!" breathed Mrs. Ray as she wiped her hands on the blue chenille.

"A fireplace that burns logs?" half-
pleaded, half-queried a thin-faced aproned
neighbor who was so new she still dragged
packing paper in her wake.

"Sure it burns logs, even coal if we put in
a grate. And the yard -- you should see it! Small
pines along one side -- only about this high now
-- but give them time, give them time. In five
years they'll be a real hedge, beautiful and real
private-like. We've got a hundred-foot lot and,
girls," she paused before dropping her bomb, "a
rock garden in back!"

"A rock garden," echoed Mrs. Ray. "Oh,
how nice! We had one at home."

"A rock garden? What's that?" added Mrs.
Lane, tilting her cigarette at a Rooseveltian
angle and hitching her trousers up a notch.

"Yes. Can you imagine it? And listen,
nothing behind me -- nothing behind me. Way
back is a nuns' home, don't know what kind,
and a long field. But nothing behind, ABSO-
LUTELY nothing but my rock garden." And Mrs.
Harrison waved her arms so forcefully that the
whole court of apartment buildings did a fade-
out a la Hollywood.

"Tell me, do you have a big kitchen?"
begged Mrs. Ray. "I do so hope it is a big one.
I've wanted one for so long."

"Well now, it's not too big. Bigger, of
course, than the ones out here. I don't know.
Well, let's see. It's longer than it is wide, something like this." And she stepped off a plan in
the dirt by the walk. "There are windows above
the sink and a back porch. And girls, listen to

me, a dining room, a decent room to eat in with the cutest corner cupboards. I can get out all my dishes again."

Mrs. Ray nodded. "I sure do like a real dining room. Especially with my boys crumbing up the place like they do."

"Yes," said the new neighbor. "I do think a dining room seems so respectable. Think of Christmas. You'll be having it in your own home this year."

"Will I! There won't be a Christmas tree nor a turkey big enough. Butchie, if you eat another doughnut you'll bust your buttons. This is the last one you get. Don't ask for any more."

"How many bedrooms in your Better Homes and Gardens?" called out Mrs. Lane.

"Now you just wait. Let me tell you about the downstairs first. You'll never believe it, but there's a big bedroom downstairs. We'll use that for a playroom for the kids. They won't have to litter their toys all over the living room. We can also put our studio couch in there."

"You can put up your ironing board in there, too," said Mrs. Ray helpfully. "You won't even need to take it down, just keep it up handy all the time."

"Why I could, couldn't I?"

"You can put your sewing machine in there, too," added Mrs. Lane. "Handy for mending."

"Is there a garage?" I wondered.

"No, but plans are made for one. All set to go. All we need is the material. And on top of the garage we'll put a sun deck, a railing around it so the boys won't fall off, of course. Just give us five years, five years in one place instead of five places in one year, and we'll have it fixed up almost perfect."

"Sounds perfect to me," I said.

"Yes, it's too good to be true. I go around with my fingers crossed all the time for fear that woman who sold it will change her mind and not go to California after all. Or maybe Al's papers won't come through, or maybe the war isn't over after all."

"Ah, you just live right," drawled Mrs. Lane. "You just live right, that's all."

"Well, probably I don't deserve such a nice place. But by golly, for four years now I've been hoping and planning for our own home. Four years I've lived all over this country. Say --" she lowered her voice, "I've bought one of those DDT bombs and I'm going to give our stuff a real whiff before I pack. I'm not going to take one single cockroach back with me, not one wobbly dirty measly old stinkin' roach! No, sir!"

"Yes, be careful," admonished Mrs. Ray, worried. "They say, let one get in and you've got 'em for good."

"Yeah, they're the same all over the country. As bad here in Washington as in Florida and Texas," yawned Mrs. Lane.

"You know, girls, Mother is so pleased. She's only twenty minutes away by bus. Same bus comes right by both houses. And you know that bedroom downstairs? On Saturday nights or anytime when Al and I want to step out she can stay with the kids and sleep on the studio

56

couch all night. Won't have to go home."

"You've sure got everything planned," remarked Mrs. Lane, "even to stepping out on Saturday nights."

"She sure does." Mrs. Ray shook her head dubiously. "Too well planned -- even to stepping out from a house she doesn't have yet. Believe me, if I had a place like that I'd never step out of it. I'd just -- well -- I'd just squat."

Mrs. Harrison was gazing off into the distance and smiling to herself. Butchie was chewing on the now empty doughnut box.

A Dream.
The Elevator That Wouldn't Go Up

This dream comes out of a stay in Paris shortly after the war when my husband had a Fulbright Fellowship to France. Frenchmen were still beginning their sentences, "Pendant le guerre." The Korean War came to make the air tense all over again. Should we flee? Where?

A Dream.
The Elevator That Wouldn't Go Up

It was in December. We were all in the car, packed and ready to start -- my husband, our daughter, our son, myself -- when I remembered two things I had forgotten to pack. My black gabardine suit and my navy polka dot dress were still up in the apartment hanging on the closet door, covered with paper wrappers just as they had come from the cleaners. Such a shame, such a bother, especially now that we were all in the car and so anxious to leave.

"It won't take long. How could I have been so careless? I'll hurry."

"Oh, Mom," the children set up a howl, "don't go back up. Let's go now."

My husband sighed and with a resigned slump to his shoulders shut off the motor of the car. I jumped out. We were in a busy narrow street much like the Rue de Vaugirard in Paris where we lived last fall. I ran across the uneven block pavement and into the dark hall of the building. The hall inside was large -- heavy stone columns supported a vaulted ceiling -- the impression was that of a public building, the actual composition was a juggled mixture a la Dali of the lower chambers of the Abbey at Mont St. Michel and the waiting room in the Grand Central Station in New York. It had the same odor as did a very ancient mouldy building on the Boul. Mich. where I had once gone in search of an apartment. My heel taps echoed and re-

echoed among the colonnades, multiplying by
compound interest my hurry.

The elevator door stood open. How lucky! I
stepped into it breathlessly. "Up," I said to the
operator, "fourth floor, *numero* 451."

The operator sat on a high stool reading a
little book. He was a medium-sized young man,
healthy, pink cheeked, wearing a grey-blue
coverall combination definitely meant for labor.
Slowly he got off the stool and with an absent-
minded air closed the elevator door.

"Okay." His voice had a pleasant drawl.
"I'll get you up there -- eventually."

The elevator was an old-fashioned cage
similar to those found in many Parisian apartment buildings, the kind of lift one operates
oneself by complicated shutting of doors, guess-
ing at correct buttons, and then praying all the
wavering journey upward. This elevator, however, was larger and sturdier. I could look out
through the bars on all sides. But I noticed that
we were not moving up, we were moving hori-
zontally along a corridor.

"Hey! *Attendez!*" I said. "What's this?"

The man in coveralls looked out through
the bars in a mildly interested manner as we
began to pick up momentum. He seemed not at
all disturbed.

"Oh," he said after a period of considera-
tion. "I think this is fun. Don't you? Don't
worry," with a wave of his arm that was
supposed to be reassuring, "I'll get you up. But I
want to go this way for a while. In case you are
not aware of it, this is a very special elevator.

Can go both directions -- up, or this way. Isn't it wonderful!"

I could not speak, but a sputtering began to simmer within me. Suddenly the elevator stopped.

"Pardon me. Have to get out here. I need a cup of coffee. Will be right back." And he stepped out and disappeared around the corner of a narrow and mysterious hallway. I thought I should get out but not knowing where I was I feared I would lose time in hunting through strange passages. I could come out on a rear street or who-knows-what labyrinth.

He came back, whistling. We moved on, skirting the side of a central court.

"Used to be a lovely garden in there," he explained. "But now ---." He shrugged his shoulders expressively. The court was entirely cemented like a drive-in of a filling station, no flowers, no trees, and the windows of the apartments that faced the court were closed and blank. There were no curtains, no window boxes, not even a mop hanging out to dry nor bottles cooling on a sill, only rows and rows of blank windows going up and up. From the elevator I could not see the top of the building nor the sky. Somewhere on the fourth floor I should be. In fact, I should be back down and away in the auto by now. I could have walked up. I certainly *would* have walked up if I had know this. What was the family thinking? They were no doubt beginning to stew. I absolutely had to get out.

But we moved slowly and steadily on. At last we stopped. We were at the edge of our building and were staring into other buildings as if from an elevated railway. My guide, as he presumed himself to be, began to point out various architectural features of the tall structure next to us. One part of its wall had fallen in.

"Commenced under Napoleon III, completed in the Third Republic, it maintains an atmosphere of elegance with all the durable features of modern French construction. Notice how the corner of that edifice still stands. No danger of its falling. Built absolutely right -- absolutely. See along there, not even a crack. Will stand five hundred years perhaps. And the facade -- you can't see it very well from here -- the facade is perfection. Such proportion of ornamentation to basic structure -- only a true artist achieves such beauty in restraint."

"But that crumbled section, all those bricks and rubble." I pointed. "That whole side of the building. What about that?"

"Not important -- not at all. *Tiens*, look at the way the corner holds. Observe that the bricks are rounded. Excellent -- excellent!"

"The last war?" I asked.

He nodded briefly and went on exclaiming over the miraculous building. I could see only half of the building. It was very much like many others. Right now I cared not one whit about its style of architecture, whether its bricks were square or rounded on the corners, and I had no interest whatsoever in the lyrical qualities of the

facade. All of this was nonsense. I had to get up
to 451.

"Please -- let us go," I begged.

So he threw the car in motion and we
began to move back. We came to the court. It
seemed different this time, as if it were an
enclosed street. Here the blonde young man got
out, tucked a square box under his arm and,
after informing me that he had to deliver a
package, again disappeared. I paced back and
forth until he returned. He came back whistling,
impervious. Once again we got underway.

At another hall, exactly like an apartment
lobby on 113th Street in New York (white tile
floor and desk by the door), we were stopped by
a man who rang the bell. He was a large man in
uniform, an Admiral with many gold stripes on
his arm. He spoke to the blonde man confidently.

"Sergeant, please help my wife and
children to the car. All these boxes and
suitcases, too."

Beside the man stood a woman in a fur
coat, three children, and a mound of baggage.
Naturally, the Admiral could not carry baggage.
I understood that. But his wife and children. I
had some children too, and I wanted desperately
to see them.

"I'm very sorry," I spoke out firmly. "I'm in
an awful rush. My family is waiting for me. It is
extremely important. Please let him take me and
then come back for you."

But no one paid any attention to me. The

young man said, "Of course."

He got out of the elevator and carried two of the children (one on each shoulder) out of the lobby. The lobby now had the appearance of the hold of an ocean liner as one faced the covered gangplank at disembarkment. Every box, every suitcase was carefully removed. The Admiral removed himself soon after his order.

When the lobby was empty the young man came back into the elevator, closed the doors meticulously, and set the car in motion. Finally we reached the first hall, the high-ceilinged entrance where I had come in. I was sick. My stomach felt as though it had become unhinged in the middle and fallen open. I was wringing my hands. What would my husband say? Would he be looking for me? What if the family would be gone when I got out to the street? Where should I wait for them? What should I do?

I don't know whether I ever got up to the fourth floor. I wonder today how many of us ever will.

Kid Stuff

Children leap and spurt in their growth. One day they are youngsters, the next day they teeter on the wire, then they are teenagers and off. This incident marked a point in our son's life more indelible than did the pencil that measured his height on the closet door jamb.

Andy's twelfth Halloween was different, somehow. He approached it routinely, with undisturbed nonchalance. Yet as the day went on something was lacking. The parade at school had not been as much fun as last year. His pirate costume had been a last-minute, hurry-up affair. The cakes with pumpkin faces at the school party were old stuff. Even orange punch wasn't much, might as well be pop. By evening, at dinner, when I asked him to walk with me and his sister Kirstin so she could meet some of her friends, his disappointment boiled up and over.

"Walk with her!" An unbelievable request. "Just so she can meet some old girls? Do I have to?"

"Well, I guess so. Daddy has the car and won't be home until late. But it might be fun, Andy."

"Fun! Gosh! And besides, if Kirstin goes I won't have anyone to go tricks or treats with."

"What about David and Jim?"

"David is going to some old church thing and Jim is having a party or something. They asked me, but it's just a bunch of little kids running around crazy."

Kirstin was excited and wanted us to hurry. She and four others were planning to collect money for the United Nations Childrens' fund. Nancy had prepared darling little collection boxes. She thought that if they went to a lot of houses they might get as much as ten dollars. Maybe her section at school would raise the largest amount.

"Why is it she always figures out something way ahead?" Andy muttered. The night was actually here and he suddenly realized that he had made no plans. He bolstered himself with a third slice of bread and jelly, but even that did not brighten him and he put down the crust.

"Surely you can find someone to join for tricks and treats. Maybe Jake. Phone him," I said. "This walk won't take long, just a few blocks. Look, we can see the moon right now from the table. Oh, it's a wonderful Halloween evening -- perfect!"

When we stepped out the door I saw again that it was a perfect Halloween. One I had often wished for when I was a girl. The moon was full, pale gold, dramatic and bewitching. The air was soft and pungent with fallen leaves and smoldering bonfires. The street lay before us as quiet and mysterious as an empty stage.

We went as far as the hedge when Andy stopped and turned back.

"I'm not going. Why, this is nothing!" And he started to run toward the house. In his old red mackinaw a little short at the wrists and his brown stocking cap jammed on one side of his head, he seemed newly tall, thin-legged and angular. Kirstin and I stood still and waited. He stopped, undecided, in the middle of the lawn, looked up at the moon, making a rebellious gesture as if throwing an armful of something away.

"Please come, Andy," I begged. I could only beg, not order. I whispered to Kirstin, "This is not easy for him." And for once she had the good sense to keep still.

He came. We walked single file, kicking the leaves as we went. I remarked about the color of the maples, bright even at night with street lights. Kirstin was polite, I continued attempts at conversation, Andy came along.

We turned into Greenwich Forest, a subdivision where the trees are taller, the houses set further back from the road, and the winding streets safe for walking. The stage became suddenly alive and we saw Halloween flitting and flickering and grinning everywhere. Parties in every block, jack-o'-lanterns in windows, little whispering figures in tall black hats, in skeleton suits, or in sheets that billowed full as they ran, a woman in a station wagon driving slowly, her passengers little girls who go out often to run up to doors, "Tricks or Treats!" A smiling father greeted us like familiar neighbors. He stood patiently at the curb waiting for three little urchins who were receiving candy at a doorstep.

"Why aren't you in costume? You won't get any loot."

We laughed with him as we passed. "Just kid stuff," Andy said, pulling up his mackinaw collar and hunching along faster. A squat, short-legged beagle ran out to the road and barked at us noisily. Andy went over to speak to him and we waited while he patted him. The little dog ran back in a spray of leaves, barking again as a gang of ghosts and witches came shouting around the corner of his house.

"Sort of cute, aren't they," said Andy, smiling for the first time.

"There are the girls," Kirstin cried happily and we hurried forward to meet them. Andy stopped, however, and said he would wait right there. The girls were bubbling with excitement over their already successful collections. I watched them go up to a well-lit rambling house and then rejoined Andy, taking his hand as we started back.

"Three blocks you said. It must be a mile," he groaned loudly. "It seems forever. I'm tired. My leg hurts." He withdrew his hand.

"Sprained my fingers again today -- in football."

As we passed an open door a woman called out to the cluster of children on her door-step, "Wait, I have California on the wire."

Andy snorted. "They always say that, 'California on the wire.' Makes it sound impor-tant."

We passed the same cheerful daddy marshalling his herd of tricksters. He nodded at us and then shook his head helplessly as a little Davy Crockett chased a gypsy maid and she fell over the sidewalk, spilling her sack of treats. The same beagle came out to greet us and Andy stopped again to pat it. Sassy at first, it became quiet and sniffed Andy thoroughly.

"Goodbye, Beagle," Andy called as we went on. "On my paper route I name the houses by the dogs they have. I have a Mad Dog house, a Toy Dachshund house, a Yappy Terrier place, and a House of the Big Dane."

We left Greenwich Forest and turned onto a busy street toward home. Two bold high school boys were walking in the road and one jumped forward a little in front of a coming car and laughed as the driver swerved to avoid him. The next car was a grey police car. It stopped beside the boys.

"A police car!" Andy was big-eyed. "They'll get it now. Last year Jake's little brother had his sack of stuff stolen by some big boys, down there by the apartment houses. They're mean, teenagers." He sniffed.

Jim yelled to Andy from his front porch as we came up our walk, "Come over."

"Naw -- not now."

We lit the pumpkin and put it in the front bay window. It was lop-sided at the back but the largest pumpkin we ever had.

"This is an awful night." Andy threw his jacket down and collapsed on the davenport. "I might as well go to bed. I'm *going* to bed."

As I hung up my coat I saw him go to the kitchen. He asked for a sack, a big grocery sack -- no sissy little baby sack. "I'm going out," he said desperately. "Even if I have to go alone."

"Alone!" I hesitated to let him go.

"Where's that dumb coat of mine? Hurry.
It'll be too late. No -- no mask. That's silly for
me. Where's the sack? I just had it. Yes, I'll stay
out only an hour and I'll go down Custer and
come back Marion Lane -- no other streets. I
promise. Goodbye."

The door slammed and from the window I
could see him running very fast across the lawn
and across the road under the street light. His
long legs which usually tangled with his heavy
shoes flashed tonight in easy rhythm. There was
a gleam of red from the mackinaw just before he
disappeared. A foreboding terror -- not of Halloween -- stunned me. But I calmed myself and
went into the kitchen to wash the dinner dishes.

I was just finishing the skillet when the
doorbell rang loudly. Another trickster, I
thought. But it was Andy, beaming at me with a
childish tease in his eye and holding the big
sack out for my donation. Then he came in
leisurely, took off his coat and hat carefully, got
a large mixing bowl from the kitchen and
dumped his loot into it. He settled himself with
a comfortable sigh on the couch and began to
sort out his candy, popcorn, apples, and
oddments on the coffee table.

"Someone asked me if I wasn't too old," he
remarked between chews of taffy. "Probably this
is my last year."

"Oh," I said.

He picked out a Mars candy bar, un-
wrapped it and ate it in three bites. "Mrs. Smith
gave it to me. Went in the dining room to get it.

Said I probably wasn't interested in the other kind. She talked an awful long time, said she was going to call on you soon. Oh, have some of this, Mom."

"No thanks, not another bite of corn candy for at least a year."

"I'm sorry, Mom. Shouldn't have eaten the candy bar, should have given it to you. I didn't think. Here, a Hershey kiss -- for you."

"Thank you very much."

"You know, Mom, it's a good thing I went out after all. You know the man across the street in the stone house? He asked me to help clean up his lawn Saturday. I said I would."

He fingered the candy, putting similar pieces in rows across the table, then he put them all back in the bowl.

"Guess I'll go to bed, Mom. Got to be up early. Patrol inspection at school tomorrow and we've got to wear our uniforms. Are my khakis clean? Should I blow out the candle in the pumpkin? No, there's still some to go. I'll leave it for Kirstin and her gang. Suppose even teen-agers like to see a pumpkin face in the window."

Listen To Brahms

I hope this incident is not embarrassing to our son who now in maturity is much less certain. Still faith in man was there, and if it did not still exist, neither would these words.

He was listening to Brahms' *Piano Concerto*. He paced the room, then dropped his full awkward length on the davenport. "Brahms is with it, isn't he, Mom? Why haven't I seen it before?"

The music surrounded us with glory. I stopped washing the breakfast dishes, poured a second cup of coffee and joined him in the living room.

"Strange, I suppose music means different things to us at different times. You can even learn about writing from Brahms," I said.

"Hear that piano. Fantastic!"

We listened.

"What do I learn about writing from Brahms?" he asked. He had become aware recently of words. He had lived on Thomas Wolfe all winter and now had found the modern poets.

"Oh, construction. How to unify and embroider a theme. And then pace -- pace is essential. To know when enough is enough. Hear him pour it on -- rich, full, almost overpowering. Then just as we are about to break he changes. He gives us exquisite lightness, pure joy. Now hear, he returns to his first statement, refreshed (and we are, too), it swells up and up into a marvelous exultation at the summit."

"Why do I find him great now when I didn't before?"

"It takes living to recognize his magnifi-

cent structure, his confidence. You have to
desire those things in your own life. I wouldn't
be surprised if this concerto is one of the
greatest achievements of our civilization."

He stooped over the record cabinet.

"Rachmaninoff's *Concerto* is here, too."

"Yes, and there to your right, an old 78
but still superb, Grieg's."

"I've got fifteen minutes before I have to go
to math class." He put on the old record. "Oh,
yes, I remember it now."

The music began, measured, cautious. It
touched us with folk cries and then overflowed
in a surge of tumult. It mounted with slow
grandeur. The waves ascended to heaven. They
probably still move toward the rim of our
universe and the edge of space.

"Music is really greater than man," he
said.

"How can it be?" I stirred my coffee.
"Music is a man-made thing, his own particular
and finite world."

"It's the silence, the great silence," he
said, pacing again. "Music goes into the silence,
off into the unknown. That's more than man
can do -- at least, yet."

"There have been several times in my life
when I could not stand music. The war years
was one." I tried to drink my coffee, but put my
hand over my eyes. "Today I realize why.
Brahms, Beethoven, Grieg, those men back
there made the music they did because they
believed that man would triumph -- even if it

were death. Start simply, try again, build higher, some may fall but others will rise, finally joy unbelievable, triumph comes. But today, who wins?"

"Why are you such a nut, Mom? Don't you know man is triumphant? Look behind you, all those books. Hear that piano. We've got to believe in man. It's disloyal not to. Sure he's just man, he's mortal, yet you've got to pull for him -- in spite of the loneliness -- in spite of the great silence out there."

He went to the kitchen and checked the clock. "Five minutes yet. Really, I guess I don't know what I believe. Here I am, almost eighteen; I've got to get a toehold pretty soon or it'll be too late. I'll begin tonight, that *History of Philosophy.*"

"There is time yet," I said, thinking of my fifty years and of my hoarded supply of beliefs.

"But where to start? Every time I think I know a piece of reality for sure it changes."

"There was Descartes, 'I think, therefore I am.' Egotistical, of course, but a start."

"I remember about him. Yes, that's right. I already believe that. But what next? Can I go further?"

"One step, perhaps," I said, speaking in careful honesty, for who was I to say? "Love is a greater force than hate."

"Well, I believe that, too. Yes, I suppose I believe that, too."

"But just when these forces are good and when they are evil, and where, and, well -- the

76

problem begins to become complicated." I drank the last of my coffee.

He opened the door. "Well, that is two things at least I believe. Goodbye now. It if doesn't rain I'll stop after class and mow the Colonel's yard. If it rains I'll come home and we'll talk some more about good and evil. But don't get discouraged, Mom. Just keep listening to Brahms!"

The Perfect One

This story began in Stockholm at a restaurant in Gamla Stan where I saw the four intriguing people described here. Who were they? The Beacham family, on the other hand, was of course not our own family. (Our daughter has the beautiful red hair, not her mother.)

Mrs. Beacham grew from part of me, part of a very self-centered friend, and portions of some universal mother who wants her daughter to become what she herself failed to become. When "The Perfect One" was finally born the question, "Who are they at the other table?" was not answered. For that I am truly sorry and apologize. But I give you Mrs. Beacham doubly strong.

The Perfect One

"This is supposed to be a typical Swedish restaurant, not three star but good," I explained to my family as we inspected the entrance of the Oaster Restaurangen on a narrow street in the Gamla Stan of Stockholm. The children made no objections, Ross because he was hungry and Betty because she was thinking only about holding Randy's hand. Gerald shrugged his shoulders and led us in. I could tell he'd have been perfectly satisfied to eat at a *Ringbanen*. Why are professors like that? The more famous they are the more indifferent they seem toward the nice things in life. I know he is embarrassed because he knows no Swedish, yet that is no reason for him to act apologetic and hesitant toward the headwaiter. All headwaiters are glad to have customers no matter what language they speak.

"Five of us," I stepped up. "*Fem*", and held up five fingers.

"Madam," he bowed and ushered us through a smog of cigar smoke to a second and more private dining room in the rear.

Betty gushed. Although nineteen she still gushes. "Mom, isn't this neat! Egg-cup candlesticks, and that tremendous red and gold rooster on the tapestry!"

Ross sneered at his sister's exuberance and winked at Randy. But I could tell he too was pleased because he suddenly remembered to hold my chair and his expression was alert instead of sulky. Young men these days are so unpredictable, rebellious one minute, bored to death the next. One must admit the world itself is a bit unpredictable. It takes strength of character to face up to it. I don't know yet about Ross. At least he is going to be handsome; already at sixteen he has Gerald's height (without his stoop) and my red hair. Good jaw, strong and firm, shows up when he isn't chewing something. There he goes, eating the relishes before we have even looked at a menu.

I seated Randy between Betty and me. Why he just happened to turn up again is obvious by now. First Paris, then Copenhagen, and now Stockholm. The Somersets must have money or else, out of desperation, they have let him go his own way. He's not bad looking, but positive, very positive. In fact, one might say he borders on the insolent. Oh, polite, too polite, he slams it in my face and forces my hand. And he's so open about his feelings for Betty. She takes it either as a joke or *un fait accompli*. Betty has not had many boyfriends, being tall and awkward like her father, and unfortunately having his light unmanageable hair, too. She'll never be a real beauty, I'm afraid.

Exactly as we were leaving the hotel, Randy appeared. "Mrs. Beacham, sure nice of you to invite me to join you," he had the grace to say, just enough embarrassment but no more. Wonder why Betty didn't warn me. Well, at least he isn't in those greasy leather shorts and dirty

tennis shoes he wore every day in Copenhagen.
Betty said he had a beard last year in college.
Imagine Mrs. Somerset made him shave it off.
He speaks of his parents affectionately, but with
a lofty paternalistic air. From Evanston; some
nice homes out there. His father is "in business," that's all I could get out of him. Could
mean anything -- even the stockyards! Betty
says he expects to be a doctor. A doctor's wife
has a hard life. Doctors, most of them, are
worked to death. And they are so narrow -- only
medicine.

I'm glad Gerald is in history, he can talk
about ideas once in a while. His students,
especially those who come to our Wednesday
teas, hang on his words. He's considered an
authority now. And he should be, all the time
he has spent on research, the family vacations
we have given up, the times we traveled, not for
pleasure but always to be near special libraries.
And even then, without the McKean money, he
might still be at his first book. Mother was right,
though. I see it now. "Gerald has it in him; all he
needs is someone to arrange things for him. Let
him work, Elizabeth," she used to say. "You'll be
proud of him some day." And I was proud today
at the Congress. He read his paper so well, he
looked perfectly right up there behind the
podium. The others congratulated him, even Sir
Charles. "A contribution, outstanding!" They all
said such nice things.

"Fish, dear?" Gerald asked. "They have
fish in every form, *fisken*. Let me see, *Helgef-
lundra* or *flax*?

I looked up from my menu and that was the moment I saw her -- the most beautiful girl in the world. So she seemed to me, and in my forty-five years I have been very observant. The girl sat with three other people at a table facing us. I stared. Here was Rimi from *Green Mansions*, hair fair and light, caught to the top of her head and then allowed to hang in frothy disorder down her back. Her face without make-up was fine-boned, her slender form shapely as a Degas ballet dancer, her eyes -- eyes once seen became the focus and all else the frame -- oblong, dark, violet lidded, drawn in a free bold stroke by Zeus or -- let's be sensible -- genetics and breeding. She coud have come from another planet, definitely another century. Henry James would have done her justice, pointing out the innocence of her simple blue dress and the black velvet ribbon holding back her hair. With hypnotic fascination he would have dwelt upon the curve of her cheek, her aura of refinement and aloofness.

The girl's mother must be a wise and clever woman to have preserved her prize un-spoiled. Her mother, yes, of course, the lady across from the girl was obviously her mother -- an immaculate well-corseted firgure in oyster white satin. Yes, the same hair, but cut short and curled under a tiny veiled hat. Yes, the same oblong eyes with violet lids. No longer the figure of a dancer but curved, shimmering, iridescent.

Beyond the mother sat another woman.

When she leaned forward I glimpsed an aging profile rising from a fluffy mass of white fox fur and topped smartly with a black tricorn hat. She too had oblong eyes, but they squinted. Her light hair was grey sand and her whole visage and person folded in upon herself and nestled into the luxury (or the security) of the fox collar. Mother, daughter, grandmother, always a fascinating sight. The same blood, yet each a generation apart. The mother round and full, the grandmother dried up, resigned, yet both relaxed and not unsatisfied, for the quintessence of their beauty still lived in certainty across the table.

Oh, I wish Mother were here, I wish she could be here. They say I am her exact image. Betty doesn't resemble me at all. Why didn't she get at least my hair? Red hair can compensate for a lot of nondescript features.

"Nice," Ross said to Randy, nodding toward the girl.

Randy turned sideways and looked. "Ah," as he nudged Betty.

"Is she worth turning around for?" Betty whispered.

"Absolutely," I said. It would be good for Betty to see the girl. Such a *spirituelle* quality is not common, certainly not on American campuses. One might find a face like that in some sheltered New England or Southern family, or in a few European aristocractic families, a few.

Betty stopped to pick up her purse from

the floor and peeked. "If you go in for lots of hair," was all she said.

"Personally, I prefer my women less breakable," said Randy as he and Betty laughed with their heads together.

"Take a load of that Jesus beard," Ross announced in a low voice.

The fourth person at the table was a slender man with a dark, well-trimmed beard which was not a determined beatnik growth or even a brave vacation gesture, but a neat fostered adornment out of the nineteenth century. In fact, the whole table was a Renoir come to life: the girl's hair, fine, flying, a little blurred; the white satin suit reflecting with an opalescent sheen the older woman's curves; the beak of the black tricorn hat a background shadow, and the man resting his chin on hand (a red signet ring showing) and gazing unhurriedly about the dining room. *Tableau.*

Gerald, who had been writing notes on the margin of his Congress program, looked up. He too glanced at the next table.

"Hmn! Who is the man in the case?" he asked.

I was suddenly very disappointed in my family. How could they be so insensitive, gauche? I point out perfection, sheer beauty, Venus rising from the sea. They see chiefly a lot of hair or a beard. In a way it has always been like this. I've spent my whole life in search of -- in a struggle for -- perfection. They have no inkling of my struggle. They do not appreciate all I

have done for them; in fact, they often openly
oppose me. Take just the physical body: pedia-
trician, shots, dentist, oculist, allergist, plus the
riding lessons, tennis and swimming lessons,
dancing lessons, and then the camps, the trips,
well ---. And whose money made possible most
of the extras? The McKean money, certainly not
a teacher's salary. The club, the summers on
the cape, the plays, the concerts. Thank
goodness the college fund is set up and secure.
No perfection is attained without drive and plan.
Mother had that drive, I got that from her, too.
"Never let down, never slump," she would say.
"Keep up the standards. They'll thank you for it
someday."

"Do we have to take the tour to Walde-
marshüdde tomorrow?" Betty asked. "Randy is
staying at the Youth Hostel and guess what? It's
that beautiful sailing ship we saw in the harbor
across from the Palace. Randy says Ross and I
could visit it tomorrow, and I'd so much rather."

Ross nodded his head at me insistently.

"I have already bought the tickets," I said.
The struggle was on again. "It's the home of
Prince Eugene. They say it is lovely. There's a
boat ride on the way."

Betty sighed and turned to Randy,
"Mother is indefatigable. She lines up the tours,
restaurants, museums -- we are educated and
cultivated in spite of ourselves. Too bad she
finds us such poor material."

Ross turned to me, "Mom, you don't
realize. This tour stuff is for old-maid school

teachers and timid guys. I just want to go out on the streets and see the people. What d'ya say, Randy?"

"Mrs. Beacham may be right," Randy gave me an honest look. I was not sure it was his honest opinion. "You get a good survey on a tour. When you figure you may never come this way again, it pays to save time. Personally, I try to do both."

"I think the man is her husband," Betty said, half to herself. Her light hair, as usual, was falling over one eye. One barrette would help.

"She has a ring on her left hand," I noticed. "But the man is too old for her."

"Swedish women wear the wedding ring on the right hand," said Randy. How he picks up such odd bits of knowledge I don't know. "But the man is much too polite to be the husband. See, Betty, the manner in which he lights her cigarette."

"Maybe he is a real estate agent and is trying to unload some place like Walder-marshüdde." Ross, always practical, suggested.

"No, that doesn't fit," I protested. "Notice, no one is trying to entertain the others. There's no wine in an ice bucket, no sharp orders to the waitress. They know each other well. See how relaxed, almost bored they look. They remind me of a short story I've read somewhere. Henry James, maybe -- tempo unhurried."

"Elizabeth," Gerald was paying attention to us at last. "Spare me Henry James. His brother, perhaps, but not Henry. A gifted snob, nothing solid. No doubt the Bostonians were glad he stayed in exile."

"But Daddy, he was assigned reading in my freshman English," said Betty.

"*Daisy Miller*," I finally had it. "*Daisy Miller*, the tale of the mother who groomed her beautiful daughter for a wealthy marriage. The bearded gentleman could be an Italian suitor."

Randy scowled. "I don't believe you've hit it yet, Mrs. Beacham. Daisy was an American girl, rather incorrigible if I remember. This girl is speaking Swedish, looks a little French, she --- . Well, take Betty here, Betty could be Daisy, she's beautiful in a vital fresh way, no hothouse plant."

Betty looked startled, taken off guard. Then she laughed, "I couldn't be Daisy Miller. Her mother was a nincompoop, not like mine, the Directrice. You'd never let me go to the Coliseum in the moonlight with an Italian count, would you, Mom?"

"Neither would I," said Randy, patting Betty's hand. "Remember what happened because of the Coliseum? Poor Daisy died."

It's been a long time since I've read James. I guess Betty really resents me. And all this has been for her own good. It began with the tennis lessons which she hated and then the dancing lessons. She even began to hate the club which we'd never have joined if it were not for Mother. Mother paid the initiation fee, exorbitant really, since once you were in the members were just like people everywhere, maybe even duller. And the French trip to improve her French; she'd never made Radcliffe without that and the extra tutoring in math. Betty is bright enough, she thinks right to the point like her father, yet she refuses to learn the most rudimentary facts about clothes, posture, how to be agreeable or persuasive. Won't let me touch her hair, cuts those ragged bangs herself. She seems to enjoy being perverse. Wonder how the woman over there managed her daughter? Now the old lady is speaking, they all lean forward to listen respectfully. Ah, what a perfect trio: the grandmother, aged but respected; the mother, a mature beauty with everything under control; the daughter, a product of skillful training and good fortune. Maybe it takes three generations to achieve some sort of perfection. And the man -- he belongs -- but where? The dark mysterious stranger, the unknown ingredient.

The waitress removed our soup and served the fish. I tried to determine the ingredients in the sauce, so delicious on the sole. Gerald has no idea how much work goes into a dinner party, not only the food, but the right people. I'll never forget my dinner last winter when President Jones offered Gerald the deanship, came right out and asked him at the table. But Gerald was emphatic, no. And I had thought all along he'd take it if offered. No administration, he said, a professorship is perfect. Prestige and money mean very little to him. I guess I'll never understand him. Time and quiet is all he wants, he says. *Who* has always taken the burden of arrangements off his shoulders? Where would he have been without me?

"I heard your paper this morning at the Congress, Dr. Beacham," Randy remarked. "I hope it will be published. If the social scientists can beat the physicists there may be hope yet for civilization."

Gerald looked pleased and began to warm up as he always does when the subject touches his field. "Some good papers at this session. A surprising number of commentaries, too. Intelligent people have been saying for some time, Randy, that it is a race between understanding and ruthless self-interest. Now national self-interest, becoming stronger all the time, enlarges the danger. But it's faulty thinking to blame the scientists. History can be used as a tool too, misused."

"Well, I hope it stays cold war and not hot," Ross put in. "I'll be up for military service in two years."

Two years! I was bathed in sudden heat. The day would come, the day would definitely come, when Ross would walk out of our lives, right out into the brutal, chaotic world. And he is grinning as if he anticipates it. And what can I do about it? What can any individual do these days? I suppose Gerald, for all his absent-mindedness, is helping to foster sanity in the world - his books are being read a little and some of his students could be a bit wiser because of his influence.

As Gerald ordered our desserts his eyes rested on the next table. Then he made a pronouncement in Hitchcock tones. "The man is the lover of the mother."

I could see the man's dark eyes upon the woman in white. She cut a piece of meat expertly and ate from her fork in her left hand, European style. Then she daintily pressed her napkin to her lips and sat back, languidly twisting the stem of her water goblet as if studying its form.

"Why do you say that?" I asked lightly, casually.

Gerald shrugged and took off his glasses and wiped them with the large table napkin. There was a dot of teasing speculation in his eye which I did not exactly enjoy.

"Obviously," he said, "he is not the father of the young girl as she resembles him in no way. He is too wordly to be interested in an affair with her, a young girl who has as yet only a flawless nose and driad hair to offer. It must be the mother, a very attractive woman. See how calmly she sits, about her is an unmistakable air of fulfullment."

Betty and Ross both laughed out loud, not shocked, only delighted to find their father so amusing. I smiled but did not say a word. Fullfillment! Foreign travel must be affecting Gerald. I've never heard him speak -- or at least seen him look quite like that. He is boldly studying the woman. She *is* sort of intriguing -- the satin

shimmers. Coeds get nowhere when they try
their wiles on Gerald for high grades. Maybe
now, in his middle years, the dangerous age, he
will change. I suppose I haven't always been the
perfect wife, but who is? There have been times
when I didn't feel even friendly. Living with a
person for twenty-three years doesn't mean you
know his inner life. Maybe I could try more. I
suppose it is possible to stereotype one's own
husband: tweed suit, pipe ashes on the floor,
roast beef for dinner, chess with old cronies,
never sell the old car as long as it runs.

Ross reached over and touched my arm,
"Don't worry, Mom. He won't leave you for Fatty
over there. Besides, I think he still loves you, in
spite of - - -."

In spite of! It should be *because* of all I've
done for him and for all of them. They seem to
be amused, not at all grateful for the patterns
I've cut out for them. Sometimes they don't even
pay attention. How hard it is to raise children!
Everything seems to be harder these days when
I thought it should be getting easier.

"Do you know what strikes me about
those people?" Randy said thoughtfully. I
noticed for the first time that his eyes were
brown. "A lesson in genetics. Had a great teacher in that last year. Old Jensen, remember him,
Betty? It's curious that those women all have
the same eyes when you realize that each one
had a different father. In any mating the female
and the male contribute the same number of
chromosomes. The probability from one particu-

lar grandparent is at most one-fourth, sometimes only one-ninth or one-tenth.

"You know, Mrs. Beacham, even though
that type doesn't appeal to me, I'll have to admit
that the girl is beautiful. Yet I can't help wondering about her father. Now, if Betty and I were
to marry we might get a throw-back who would
have red hair like yours. Unfortunately, red hair
is recessive, Betty. Still, with perhaps one-fourth
of Dr. Beacham's brains, your red hair, and
Betty's wonderful figure, disposition and all," he
gave Betty a frankly appraising glance, "plus my
athletic form and a few minor advantages too
numerous to mention," he flexed one arm in a
muscle-raising stunt, "who knows, ours might
be the perfect one!"

Betty felt his biceps and they all laughed
as if it were a marvelous joke. It was not funny.
Nothing was funny. How foolish to think I could
control. There is always, as Randy said, another
-- always the dark, mysterious stranger. Randy
has done something else. He is too young to
realize how it hurts. He has shoved me over. I no
longer sit in the luminous satin but have put on
the white fox fur and the tricorn hat.

I felt a buzzing in my ears. It was quite
loud. It was the sound of all my nice arrangements toppling off the shelf. I sat very still and
held my breath, praying that some small part of
me would survive the falling debris.

A Mother's Dream

This dream is recounted here, not for its psycho-analytical implications but for its symbolism. At different stages in my life I have had such dreams, dreams that might make a great series of surrealist drawings.

(The reader might be interested to know that in recent dreams I am about to miss an airplane, not a train. So, in my subconsciousness I move with the times.)

A Mother's Dream

It was summer and Monday morning. We were leaving our weekend cottage to catch an early train back to the city. The cottage, a family building project, never seemed to be done. We hated to leave it, but urgency was thick in the air. Someone held up a board and someone pounded in the last nail. Then the screen door slammed and we were on our way.

My husband was dressed for the office in dark suit, white collar, tie. He carried his black leather briefcase and strode along steadily. I wore a grey dress with a matching jacket, a dress long since given to the Salvation Army and forgotten, but now that it comes to me out of the past it was a very useful dress indeed. Our son and daughter sauntered behind us, stopping to look at various rocks and picking black-eyed susans. With the early sun lighting her strawberry blonde hair, our daughter seemed already mature in outline; our son, younger and appealingly awkward, was just beginning to shoot up to his final six feet. They were companions, full of secrets and mysterious plans.

The way to the railroad station was not a smooth tree-lined country path but a shortcut over rough terrain. I walked carefully, zigzagging and picking my path to avoid turning an ankle on the uneven gravel. Once when I turned back I could see the cottage deep in an English landscape painting far, far away. Our children were slowing, dallying, laughing at something they were saying to each other. We carried no suitcases; *"voyagers sans baggage."* At the top of the hill my husband stopped and motioned strenuously for the children to come on faster. I shouted at them. They shouted back and waved.

Our steps resounded on the worn cobble-stones as we hurried across a large plaza in front of the railroad station. The morning air held rising steam from sun on cool stones, a smell of coffee, yes, the smell of browning coffee beans one awakens to in Rome. People were buying newspapers, *Figero* and *Le Matin*, at a kiosk. But no, this must be France. Once again turning back I could see the tops of our children's heads as they came up the hill, a glint of strawberry blonde and a tuft of unruly yellow. My husband and I went into the station.

It was the Gare Montparnasse of twenty years ago. "I have to be there at nine," my husband said. "I have their tickets," I said. "I'll have to go on," he said. "I'll wait," I said. "We'll try to catch you. Yes, of course you have to go."

I stood in the center of the high entrance salle with its many arches, doors coming in from the street, doors leading to the quais and the trains. Signs flashed above the doors to the quais. At a far door in a long line of commuters I saw a man in a dark suit carrying a briefcase. He handed his ticket to a collector sitting on a high stool, the collector punched the ticket. Then the man disappeared. I waited for the children but more and more people surrounded me, walking purposefully, robot-like to the trains. They wore trench coats, they carried newspapers folded neatly under their arms, they did not speak. The station was filled with the roar of their passage.

I had heard this noise before -- the tramp of commuters coming up the ramp at Grand Central Station -- the beating pulse of the thousands that hurry through the Paris subway at the Châtelet -- the scraping of soles on cement at the shuttle in Times Square -- the clap clop of feet in the packed corridors of the subway in Tokyo. I tried to keep my balance but the crowd kept pushing me along. I stretched my neck to keep my eyes on the brick archways through which the children should come. The roar increased and I awoke.

Afraid to move, I came slowly back to consciousness -- exhausted. Slowly too, I understood that no matter how long I had waited in the station they would not have come. They will never catch up. I should not want them to. I go over the dream for the hundredth time -- the arm that held the board, the screen door that slammed, the sun behind strawberry blonde hair, the man who walked in a straight line, and myself, in a grey travel dress, turning and twisting and trying to breast the crowd as I waited at the Gare Montparnasse.

Three Days at the Shoreham

When we lived in Washington a very busy couple we knew spent a weekend every spring away from their family. They went to the Shoreham Hotel and talked over all their problems. From this germ the story sprouted. In a sense it helped me in my approach to "Woman's Lib" before it was an actual social movement.

The couple pictured at the end of the story are like a man and woman I saw often at the Library of Congress. I vowed then that such remarkable individuals should be preserved.

Three Days at the Shoreham

1

"Anything you want, the Shoreham has
it," said the bellboy, unlocking the door of an
end suite on the sixth floor. "Air conditioning
adjusts here. If you prefer, I can open these." He
opened French doors onto a narrow balcony.
The warm, pleasant breeze flowed in. "Thank
you, Mr. White, thank you very much, sir. Call
Room Service anytime."

"Don, it's magnificent!" Barbara dashed
into the bedroom. "A dressing room, too. What
elegant spreads -- and those immense lamps!
Did you see the price posted by the door? Really
we don't need a whole suite. Why this bedroom
is larger than our living room. Here -- I'll take
the drawers on this side and you can have
those."

Don put his suitcase on a low rack. "Before we unpack we ought to do something to
celebrate." He kissed her lightly. "A drink? I'll
ring for ice and -- here's a card on the dresser --
Old Crow, no Virginia Gentleman, perhaps a
bottle of J.B., too. Well, Barbie, here we are -- all
this and each other too for three whole days."

"Let me see the letter again. And the
check!" She stepped out of her pumps and
flopped on a bed. "Father writes well, almost
lyrical. 'A stereo set, a new washing machine, a
silver service? More to be treasured than these
is time -- time together. This we offer you upon a
golden platter. A suite is reserved for you at the

Shoreham Hotel for three days. Sign what you
need to your room and fill in this check when
you leave. Mother and I will stay with the
children. Congratulations on your tenth anniversary.' "

"Wonderful parents." She stretched out
her arms and lay flat upon the bed. "How did
they guess I was so tired? I'm going to stay right
here for three days and not move."

"Mind if I join you?" He reached down to
grab her ankle.

"Not literally." Barbara jumped up and
walked to the dressing table. "Ten years." She
leaned close to the glass. "A grey hair, see!"

He came up behind. "In my opinion you
have improved. I remember the first time I saw
you -- red hair, long and messy, tight black
Levis dribbled with paint. Touchy as a rabbit
you were."

"Who wouldn't be touchy? 'Paint sample?'
you asked. You didn't have to insult my painting to gain my attention. You weren't so much to
look at either, as I recall, Professor White. You
looked just what you were, lowest paid member
of the history staff. Yet, after ten years," she
gave him a pat on the chin, "your rank has
definitely improved but not your appearance.
You still stoop, your teeth are yellow, your
glasses are thick. You old thing."

He straightened his tie before the mirror.
"Some of my students seem to find me attractive, at least the girls who need a C to make a
sorority."

She began to undo her hair, piling amber

pins in one of the glass ash trays. "If we are dining on the Terrace you'd better reserve a table. I'm
going to take a long, long luxurious bath -- maybe
wash my hair too."

"Your hair! Surely not now."

"Darling, you don't understand. It's been a
terrible rush -- groceries to get, one last washer to
do, a list of meals for Martin, Eunice's cat to bring
home from the vet's, Donnie's music lesson, and a
million other things. And then, when I was shaking the dust mop I saw a Japanese beetle on the
roses -- so early in the season, too. What did we
use last year for those beetles? Well, now I'm
going to shed all my grime, rejuvenate the wreck,
anoint my head with oil before my cup runneth
over."

"O.K., O.K. I'll order the flowing cup. Join
me as soon as you can, Mrs. White. Why women
have to save up everything for the last minute I'll
never understand. No organization." He went
stiffly into the other room.

When she did join him he was surprised to
see she had been crying. She came out wearing
her dove grey silk kimona, brushing her auburn
hair that hung like Rima's cloud around her. He
had waited a long time, sipping his drink and
staring out of the window at the string of evening
traffic that surged up out of Rock Creek Park and
paused for the lights at the top of the hill. From
above the cars were like rows of Martin's toys. It
was strange not to be in that fight to get home. He
felt aloof, lonely. He remembered the books he
had brought home in his briefcase. But this
weekend was not for work. It had seemed wonder-

ful in anticipation, but . . .

"Ready, dear?" He could see she was not.

" Soon. Don, I'm so blasted tired, don't
know what's the matter. The bath should have
revived me. See, I even did my nails. But I don't
want dinner and dancing, I want to crawl under
the covers and just stay there. Oh, they brought
the drinks. Yes, it might help. Funny, I miss our
own house -- humble though it be."

She pattered around in bare feet looking
at the pictures and turning on lamps. "Candles
in sconces, too rococo. They all need straighten-
ing. At home we have real candles." She tore up
a paper cocktail napkin and wrapped the bases
of the wooden candles and put them in straight.
"This is all very lovely, don't you think?"

"You've said that several times." He
handed her a Scotch. "It is lovely when you are
in it. Otherwise it could be anywhere for me ---
a desert island."

"Luxurious island, I'd say." Tears came
unexpectedly and she ignored them. She tried
her drink as if it were medicine. "I feel a breeze
from the balcony. Let's sit on the floor and enjoy
it. Dry my hair, too. We were married at eight
o'clock. A hot night, warmer than tonight."

"You were beautiful then, more beautiful
now," he toasted her.

"After three children, you still say that?"

"Of course, Plutarch said a woman doesn't
begin to take shape until twenty-seven."

"I'm as shapely as I'll ever be. Or am I?"

She leaned against him lightly. She
brushed her hair slowly up and out to hasten its

drying. "I go along every day doing the thing that has to be done next. No time to stop -- to ask why. But Don, I miss them, the children and all those things I must do next. I'm a kite bobbing in the sky with the string cut. I'll dive down and smash without someone holding the string. Or else," she took a long drink and sighed, "Or else I'll drift off into the wild blue yonder."

"Before you do that we'll go down and eat." He pulled her to her feet. "Need some ballast. Fifteen minutes?"

Donald could not understand even after ten years why it took thirty.

"How much we miss being stuffy stay-at-homes," Barbara said, looking about the crowded dining Terrace. "All these people, the gaiety. Notice how the lights on the fountains keep changing. Who is the young man who spoke to you, the old Princeton haircut? He's sitting near the railing with the pretty blonde."

"Denver Adams, graduate student. He may be my first Ph.D. Surprised to see him here. The girl's a charmer."

"All in ice blue, even long kid gloves. Her jeweled snood is the right touch."

"They're certainly absorbed. Wonder how serious it is?"

The waiter poured the last of their champagne solicitously.

Barbara sighed, "Nine-thirty. We were married and standing in the reception line. The church wasn't air-conditioned. Hot, wasn't it? But I was shivering. Remember?"

"I'll never forget." He held up the goblet, "Here's to fifty more."

"Fifty! We'll be in our 80's. You'll be Emeritus Professor from Harvard or someplace grand. I'll be -- well -- emeritus or emeritae something. Would you honestly want to see ahead, though, if you could?"

"I've often wondered. As a historian I'd have quite a drop on all the other chroniclers. More than that, I'd have a real basis for judging the present. But if I saw a Republican victory -- a war with China -- no one would believe me. Besides, the next generation of scholars wouldn't thank me. As Carl Becker said . . ."

"Darling," she touched his arm, "your philosophy is wasted on me tonight. Tonight is now, not ten years ago or fifty years ahead. Let's dance."

He danced evenly but with no change of step. The crowd jostled them and he worked back toward their table.

"Pinch me," she whispered. "I don't believe I'm me. Even the stars are out in our honor. Stars here, too. Isn't that man -- bushy hair and string tie -- a Senator from Texas? The twisty brunette, the French perfume who just gouged me with her spiked heel, probably the mistress of the Ambassador from . . ."

"You impress easily, my dear. These are mostly men with expense accounts. From the way they dance they're all mad. Let's go back to our table."

"There's someone you know, in the white coat. Why do you look away?"

"She's not his wife. I don't want to
embarrass him."

"Why, Don, how exciting! No, how sad."

She pulled her white stole around her
shoulders. The noise did seem excessive. A large
man leaned over their table, turnng to her.

"Barbara, little red-headed Barbara Walton. Fancy meeting you here. Jerry, Jerry Bas-
comb. Remember?" He held out his hand.

"Why, Jerry, I do remember you. It's hard
to see in this dim light. My husband, Dr. White."

"Doctor? Nice going. Mind if I take her for
a turn around the floor, Doc?"

"Thanks, Jerry," she put in hurriedly. "Not
tonight. We're celebrating -- our wedding anniversary."

"Congratulations," he still leaned on their
table. "Haven't seen you in ten years. Look just
the same. Still a little uppity, but style, boy! Still
paint, Barbie? You were going to be a Lady Rem-
brandt."

"Paint nursery walls now. I'll wait and be
a second Grandma Moses."

"I'm still in Rockville, my father's law firm.
By the way, what kind of doctor are you? Oh, a
college professor. Took a shot at the academic
grind once myself, but gave it up. I could soon
see it meant only small potatoes for me. Well,
nice to've seen you."

Don stood up but did not offer his hand.
The man went off to the dim region across the
dance floor.

"Nice guy. Boy friend?" he asked.

"Once." She shrugged. "Funny he turned

up tonight. At least ten years since I've seen him."

"Regrets?" Don asked, lighting his pipe.

"He's starting to get bald. I'd have been the wife of a rich lawyer, had three children, lived on River Road. It could have been worse." She patted his hand teasingly.

The student and his girl danced near them and stopped a little awkwardly at their table.

"Dr. White," young Adams said, "I've been telling Jean all about you and the seminar."

Don offered to get them chairs but they would not stay.

"I just wanted to say, Mrs. White," smiled the young man, "that I enjoy working under your husband -- he sure makes us dig. By the way, Professor White, I found a lead at the L.C. yesterday. You know the papers of old man Robinson have just been given to the Library. They'd be right down my alley."

Don nodded. "Come into my office next Tuesday, about noon."

As they moved away Barbara mused, "Sweet, aren't they? Were we so obviously in love?"

"Adams is a comer," Don said, relighting his pipe. "Fine showing in his prelims. Promise -- real promise. Believe I can get him access to those papers. Maybe enough material for a dissertation. Mearns would be the one to see."

He puffed away on his pipe, very well pleased. He suddenly asked for the check and signed it with a flourish. "No need to stay longer, is there?"

This is not fair! Our beautiful weekend!
Barbara switched on the bedlight briefly to look
at her watch. *One o'clock, Don still downstairs.
Not drunk? Not like him. "A fine wife," he threw at
me when he went out. What does a man expect?
If a woman doesn't feel like it she doesn't feel like
it, anniversary or not.*
*Where did the evening begin to go off?
Jerry? Hardly. Dinner was fun, so was the walk
afterwards. When we came up I started to talk
about the children. Don said, "You're here, not
home." What I wouldn't give to see them -- Eunice
lining up her dolls in their beds beside her,
Donnie sleeping with his fireman's hat on the bed
post, and Martin, so huggable. My darling, I
love ...*
There was a sound. The door. She pulled
the sheet up to her ears. Don whispered, "Barbara?" She did not move. He sat on his bed
taking a long time with his shoes. He came over
and touched the bulge of her hip. She breathed
slowly and regularly. He sighed and went back
to his bed.
She could hear the sheet rattle as he
pulled it up, then tossed it off. Even as she
listened with ear extended, he fell asleep. She
relaxed gratefully and felt herself drifting, slip-
ping, flying like Donnie's kite, up and up. Don's
breathing became louder and he snored. Then
he breathed normally. Then he snored. She tried
to lie limp, but now her body was tense. Man,
the male, snores away; woman keeps watch.

The house could burn down, he would snore on. The male animal -- arrogant, dominant, aggressive, sanctified in his righteousness, blissful in his self-esteem, secure forever in his role of lordship, rushing forward leaving the female to pick up the pieces. Barbara turned over angrily and kicked against the cool sheet. *They are all alike, only some more so.* The snoring continued and she sat up in bed dizzily. Could the champagne work twice? No, she was only mad. She slipped out of bed and into the other room, making her way by light from the street below.

From the window she could see a man and two women at the bus stop on Connecticut Avenue. A doorman, epaulets gleaming, walked to the parking lot, got into a black Cadillac and drove it slowly toward the hotel entrance. Even at this late hour cars still spurted up out of the Park and music still sounded from the Terrace. *The world goes on and I stand here -- miserable, a monstrous whale lying in the next room snorting and frolicking in his blissful arrogant maleness. But what can I do? What can any woman do? We are trapped, strapped into our roles. We start out thinking we are free, then the gates snap shut.*

An ice cube clinked in the ice bucket as it melted. She filled a glass with ice and held its coolness against her lips. *I don't really hate men, especially Don. No reason, no reason that could be written in a sentence or said in words. Don's wonderful sometimes -- when he isn't so pigheaded sure he's right, so blind at times to the rest of us. He loves me. I should be thankful instead of mad. Then why do I feel trapped?*

Jerry remembers me as an artist. What am I really? Mother, housekeeper, chauffeur, seamstress, hostess, typist? Another suburban housewife? The ice melted as she sucked on it. The light through the front window streamed across the room and flared up from her rings. "With this ring I thee wed." Ten years, ten years Don and Barbie.

But surely I am something separate too. When all the husks are peeled off -- the cook, the shopper, the laundress, the wife -- there must be a piece of me still left. Maybe there isn't. Maybe that is why I am so upset. With my props gone I fall down. I have no core.

She contemplated her toes. They were shapely, like a child's. She walked around digging them into the deep pile of the rug. *The real I must be somewhere beneath all these layers. I was there the day I walked across the platform to receive my diploma; I was there at my first fraternity dance, the belle of the ball; I was there with my first job in the art department, eagerly rushing to please; I was there when Don first stood beside me as I was putting up the show in the student Union; I was there ten years ago tonight, that funny motel near Baltimore with the rice on the floor; I was there when our first-born came, too fast, and I heard his cry. I am here tonight, Barbara Walton White, no one else.*

A quiet came. Cars ceased rushing, no one waited at the bus stop. Barbara stood very, very still with her arms clasped tightly around herself. *I am a vessel that life flows through. Is that all? Maybe more. Life might be a wee bit better because it passed my way.* Her kite in the sky steadied. She padded silently back to bed and fell soon asleep.

2

Don awoke at his customary hour of seven; he showered, shaved, and went down to the lobby for a morning paper. Barbara was still sleeping when he returned. He ordered breakfast sent up.

"Barbie," he said softly in her ear when the table was ready in the living room. "Barbie, breakfast."

She sat up straight and began automatically to braid back her hair. "What time is it? How awful! No, how blissful!" And she dropped back.

Curled up in her robe on the davenport, a second cup of coffee on her knee, she glowed. "Darling, this desert island has a magic tablecloth. And the flowers -- sure you didn't order them? The card says, 'Compliments of Archie Richmond, Manager.' "

"I don't understand it either." Don reread the card. "This morning the elevator man said something to me about 'madame, the actress,' and I said you were accustomed to late breakfasts, if any. Do you suppose when we spoke French to each other in the elevator they...?"

Barbara rose and swept across the room. "And Monsieur, what are you doing in my room if you are my manager."

109

"But, of course," Don bowed, "only a husband could be strong enough to direct such a person of temperament."

"*Touche*, please hand me my engagement book. Ah, this I shall *canceller*. Tell the press no interviews until Monday. And no fittings, they bore me. Today, today I shall direct my own hours. A walk in the park, yes, no. *Dejeuner*, no, my figure. But tea on the terrace facing the fountains, tea and little croissants and you, Monsieur, at four o'clock. The remaining minutes I shall stay to my bed, reading my part. It needs much refining."

"*Comme vous voulez*," Don hunted for his pipe among the breakfast cups. "When do I hear you read your lines?"

"Tomorrow. This is my day, mine all alone. Solitude, *delicieux*."

"But this is *our* weekend. Have you forgotten?"

She turned dramatically at the door. "No, I've not forgotten. But how can it be ours until I know what is *I* first?"

"Don't you think this actress business is going too far? Poses are too damned easy for you -- always the artist, the bohemian, now I suppose it is the breathless mother, bearing all the burdens. Barbara, there is more to life than taking up roles and dropping them."

"But those aren't roles. They are me at certain times. I want to know if they are going to add up to something." She stood with her hands over her eyes, tense.

"Well, the last ten years have added up to

quite a bit, I'd say: job, three children, house. It wasn't easy. What more do you want, Barbara?"

She took her hands from her eyes and stared at him. "What more do I want -- in the next ten years? By then Donnie will be leaving to go to college. You may be a full professor. But I, I'll probably be just as I am, no more. I'm just a -- I don't know -- a servant -- someone other people use. I give and give and am drained away until I am empty. Already I fell exhausted. If you ask me, marriage is a trap."

He worked at lighting his pipe and strode over to the window. Below him a Park policeman, mounted on a sorrel horse, galloped rapidly up the hill and turned at the top to survey the area. The animal's coat glistened like water in a mountain stream; its neck curved, its tail arched, it pranced nervously as the rider reined it to a halt. "All life is a trap, Barbie. And we must learn how to maneuver in the little space we are allotted."

"You and your philosophical generalizations! I expected somehow that after we were married life would enlarge, open up"-- she flung out her arms in a dramatic gesture, "but it seems to close us in instead."

"It could open up," he said, still watching the horse and rider. "I suppose one has to work at it."

"Thanks," she said at the door. "I shall study my part. See you at tea, Monsieur le Professeur," and she shut the door firmly.

Over his part Don was still deliberating at

midnight. The day had evaporated as if time, when not marked by its usual requirements, had been discontinued. Tea on the upper terrace had been charming. Barbara had gazed at the fountains and smiled while he read the afternoon papers. Dinner in the elegant Palladium Room has been pleasant. They had sauntered through the lobbies, stopping at a little table for liqueurs and watching the dancing from a distance. An air of detachment enveloped them. Formal to the point of elaboration they retired, each assuring the other that they were having a wonderful time.

Don stayed awake. He had mulled over his problems all day -- his book, still only half done, his chances of a professorship, the inadequacy of his life insurance, the years still necessary to pay off the mortgage, the research he would have to do before he could begin the sequel to his present book. He had made a list, several lists.

And what about Barbie? She wanted to study her part, she said. Like all women she is always wanting something. Take furniture. She said this spring they had all they needed and within a week she began talking about a piano for Donnie -- an ugly, battered corner cupboard she had seen in an antique shop -- a heavy white iron settee for the back yard. He visualized himself pushing and sweating and shoving a stack of furniture two stories high. It isn't fair, he muttered, turning again in his bed. Men spend their lives earning money to let women indulge in "things", "things." Why not just a table, bookcase, stove and bed?

He tried to make out the time on his wristwatch. It was either two o'clock or ten after twelve. He got up quietly and moved into the other room. He found his pipe and stepped out on the balcony.

Saturday night. Still a stream of traffic through the Park. *Amazing so many people still up. If, as a historian, I could only put all those activities, hopes and dreams, all that great milling mass of humanity in a pattern. But maybe I ought to leave the patterns to the sociologists and concentrate on one man -- the unique human experience. Well, that's what I'm doing in my biography. But even in a biography you have to see the life whole before the pieces fit into a pattern. One has to always be looking both ways, fore and aft.*

I wonder if I can see the Washington Monument from here. No, too bad. Barbie doesn't realize the dedication, the long hard haul, the slow accumulation that leads up to scholarship. She's impatient, jumps at conclusions intuitively, like an artist, I suppose. No way to pass a history exam. She wants the summary, never the hard work that goes before.

Women! Women! Smiling, sleek, secretive as cats. They demand, demand, grab off the cream. They tantalize you, rile you, excite you. They take, take, take, and think a man should be pleased just to give. Bearing children they smugly think of themselves as the fundamental - as if it doesn't take two. When they are teenagers they walk three abreast across the sidewalk and

*think their sex excuses bad manners; when they
are middle-aged they drive Cadillacs in the
middle of the road and wear ridiculous hats and
terrorize you with their snap opinions; when they
are dowagers they noisily demand attention and
inevitably walk to the head of a waiting line.
Ignorant, insensitive, busy at trivia.*

Three women emerged from the hotel
entrance carrying shopping bags. Their dragging
footsteps and high voices came up to him on the
balcony. *Probably cooks or chambermaids going
home. What was it Barbie said, "I'm just a servant." Not true, of course. Yet maybe I'm not
looking at her side. Surely she feels a partner in
this deal. Went into it willingly, as I did. Yet,
maybe we are each working off in our own
direction and aren't connecting. There must be a
division of labor -- but goals should be in common.*

Don took up his life objectively. The work
of the last ten years, when primary sources were
painstakingly consulted, did not equal the total
he somehow assumed. Job, children, house,
book, a rung up the ladder. But Barbie. Had he
been blind to her real desires? He assumed they
were the same as his. Perhaps there were others
-- her art, maybe. She was really a joyous
woman, pointing out beauty and fun he missed
altogether. Could he be selfish? A man has to
get ahead in this world and he did like his work.
Yet, he could make a fresh start as far as Barbie
was concerned, and the children.

He closed the French doors and marched
himself back to bed. Even though much was

lacking the length of his life was, after all, only about half over. Direction was obvious. There was promise, yes, there was promise. With a sense of equilibrium. neither accomplishment nor defeat, just a strong wind and a steady keel, he fell asleep.

3

Don felt a soft tickling across his eyes and nose. Without moving a muscle he gained awareness. Barbara was in bed with him. Curved against his back he felt her strong lean body, her breasts against his shoulders, her legs tucked bchind his. She was gently passing her pony tail across his eyes. He got a whiff of shampoo. In a second he would rise up and grasp her roughly. Last night -- last night -- and his vigil came back. *No, I can't take her, I can't take her like this. Freud be damned. It must be a result of, not a cause of, for us. If I could only see more clearly what I am and she is. O.K. I'm an animal, sure. But I'm an animal buried under layers of last nights and last nights.* With a mighty sigh he flopped over on his stomach.

What he said to the pillow Barbara could not tell, for with the lightness of a darting dragonfly she was away. He heard the water running in the tub and mumbled again. When she came back he was up.

They ate breakfast in the Garden Room where the sun poured through high windows and waitresses moved quietly. Barbara dropped her napkin and was surprised to be supplied

115

so quickly with another.

"Just think" she said, "we have time to read the Sunday *Times* at breakfast. No chins to wipe, no need to say 'drink your orange juice.' Darling, I don't even have to get up to pour you a second cup of coffee."

He nodded. "Want the book reviews?"

"Thanks. I'm always afraid something wonderful is going to be written and I'll miss it altogether. Skim the cream, but never taste the milk."

A photographer with a bulging lens on his camera stopped beside them. "May I?"

"On Sunday morning?" Don said, astonished. "How can you?"

"You should know, Mr. Whitelow. Isn't that the name of one of your plays?"

"I don't write plays, man. What an idea. You are mistaken."

"Your picture, nevertheless. There, thank you very much."

Barbara had smiled and turned her head, furnishing an attractive profile. Her motion surprised Don. Yet, in her light green suit and her madonna coiffeur she could well pose as the wife of a celebrity.

"Whitelow?" She frowned. "Oh, I know. Geoffrey Pierce Whitelow, the Englishman. How ducky!" She giggled. "He had a play on Broadway this spring. He's in Washington for a literary conference at the Folger."

Don took up the paper again. Hell! If Barbara wanted to be a French actress he might as well be a playwright, it made as much sense.

116

But what about the script? It couldn't be his alone. "Well, I wonder what Reston has to say today. The world drama goes on whether I write history or plays."

They walked in the park following Rock Creek as it flowed sluggishly around giant boulders. In the clearings the sun baked into their backs, making the shade in turn seem doubly welcome. A large man passed them along the bridle path on a cantering horse. He saluted Don gravely.

"Who was that?" Barbara asked. "I've seen that massive face, so deadpan, before."

"Dean Jorgenson. Hardly recognized him in a sport shirt. We went to his wife's funeral last fall, remember? His children are grown. I understand he is a very lonely man."

She sighed as they walked to a bench. "I don't want to think of sadness. This is a June day like no other. I remember coming here as a little girl. Let's have a picnic next Sunday before it gets too hot to cook out. We can bring Martin in his stroller."

Don dusted off the bench before they sat down. "I've been thinking," he began casually, "ten years from now, what we might be. I see some changes we could make."

"If we think of what we were ten years ago," she said, "then we can see how much we have already changed. I certainly was a dope. Still am . . ."

He put his arm on the bench behind her. "Don't worry, I'm a dope too. Strange how what we really are depends so much upon what we see both ahead and behind. Ten years is a good point in a marriage to take direction. One thing is certain . . ."

A strange couple came slowly through the filtered sunlight. The woman walked with a great lurch; her left shoe had a six-inch sole. Though the day was warm she was enveloped in a loose black-and-white plaid coat that swayed back and forth with each step. Her hair was pulled into a severe little bun. The man, nattily dressed in a tweed sport jacket, walked stiffly erect and carried a cane. The woman kept one hand upon the man's arm for support. They paused almost in front of the bench. The woman held her free hand out to the sun and said something in an animated manner. Her face was radiant; the man continued to nod. It was then they saw the man was blind.

Barbara gasped. It seemed to take a long, long time for the two to pass. For another long time Barbara could see the man's straight back, the woman's bobbing walk and her face turned up eagerly as she talked. Don's arm tightened around her shoulder. They said nothing until the swaying coat, a distant banner, disappeared with a bend in the path.

The Voice of
St. Martin-du-Bois

In the 60's we and our children spent a wonderful summer in Paris. At a bus stop one day we met an American who was studying organ under the old master, Marcel Dupré. He told us that in early September Dupré would be back at his regular post at St. Sulpice. We went to hear him. St. Sulpice is massive, cold and grey, but that Sunday as Dupré played, its stones became living and the air vibrant. That overwhelming, almost excruciating experience was a revelation to me of the totality of the human effort that had made the moment, the church, the reverberating pulsing sonority possible.

To capture this vision, which although borne on music is far more than sound, became my ambition from that day forward. This story carries my offering.

The Voice of St. Martin-du-Bois

I parked in the square directly in front of the old church and we rested a minute before getting out. The drive down from Paris had been easy. Sunday morning traffic unusually light, weather perfect for June.

"So this is St. Martin-du-Bois," I said to Sauvin. "The church where you were baptized."

Sauvin got out, keeping his eyes on the church towers, squinting against the high noon sun. I handed him his portfolio. He glanced around the square, sniffing the air.

"Smell it, Jean. Baking bread. Now you know the flavor of all the villages of France. We'll have a coffee over there at Suzanne's if we have time. First, I must try the organ."

Sauvin is thin and worn. No one would guess to look at him that he is seventy-eight. No one would guess either that he is the greatest organist in France, some say in all the world. With reservations, of course. But he is good or I'd never have come all the way to France to study under him. I'm not too bad myself -- all the pupils I can handle and a full booking of concerts for next winter. Sauvin is cagey, he doesn't give me much criticism. I jumped at the chance to drive him down when I heard about the dedication. Besides, this was my first opportunity to see the French country-side. I found it surprisingly peaceful, charming in a simple rural way, as the guidebooks say.

A stocky fellow hurried from the church

toward us. Stopping two steps away he bowed with an old-fashioned jerk, "Monsieur Sauvin, our dear gracious Monsieur Philip Sauvin, it is my great honor to greet you and to conduct you to the organ."

Sweat stood on his high forehead. He fixed his bulging eyes upon old Sauvin and waited. He was definitely not the mayor; his ill-fitting black suit and lack of tie denoted a minor functionary, no more.

Monsieur Sauvin put his hand upon the man's arm. "You are Pierre, Pierre Bastion, of course. You have cared for our church as long as I can remember. This is Jean Hamilton, an organist from the United States. He so kindly drove me here."

"A great day for St. Martin's," I said, trying to say something appropriate. My French is definitely not *rapide*.

"But certainly," Pierre replied, at attention, and obviously trying to be official. "Seldom does Monsieur Sauvin return to the place of his birth. Never have we had such an illustrious gathering in our village, not even for the marriage of Marie, the Countess du Bois. And today the great event, the marvelous unbeliev-able event has finally, after eight hundred -- permit me to be more accurate -- after a thous-and years, come to pass. St. Martin has an organ! The flooding of the foundations has been conquered and dampness is no longer our problem. The fund has been raised and the instrument installed. Now our magnificent church has at last a voice and the greatest

organist in France -- permit me to say in all the
world -- has arrived to play it for the dedication!
Yes, you are right, Monsieur Hamilton, this is a
great day for St. Martin-du-Bois."

He led us up three or four stone steps
toward the church, a fortress of a building,
certainly not beautiful, more like an American
armory except for two squared-off towers. I
noted cars parked under the trees across the
square and people closing up some booths,
apparently the village Sunday morning market.
Men in black suits were sitting at sidewalk
tables under Suzanne's orange awning. Across a
humped-up bridge right off the square was a
grassy riverside park where children were feed-
ing ducks. The main road ran on up a hill and
curved toward an old chateau, probably that of
Marie, the Countess du Bois.

"The Bishop himself will be here," Pierre
was saying as he halted before the big central
doors. "The mayor's luncheon for you will com-
mence at twelve-thirty exactly. They say the
entire choir from the conservatoire of Touraine
will come in a bus." He ran his hand over the
heavy iron braces, shaped like giant anchors,
which reenforced the thick wooden doors. "We
will open these doors this afternoon, the first
time since Easter. The wood is still good,
original, twelfth century. But yes, I have had the
workmen cross-piece it on the inside."

Pierre stepped back to gaze affectionately
at the facade of St. Martin-du-Bois. A row of
battered saints were lined up in high relief
above the doors and what looked like part of a

cow stood beside them. Maybe a coat of paint or something would improve the old doors. Sauvin looked at the church too, saying nothing, kneading his hands together, on his face an aloof expression, holding himself in readiness. I was glad to hear they were giving him the VIP treatment, for he was doing this concert for love, not even expenses. He'd rate five thousand a concert in New York any day.

The inside of the church was abruptly cool after the hot cobblestones, so dark at first I couldn't adjust my eyes. It smelled mouldy, as I guess all old churches do. Pierre directed us up a winding stairway to a balcony above the entrance. There sat a shiny two-manual console with its pipes installed behind it and at each side. The one I use back home has three manuals and over two thousand pipes. But these little organs have lots of power and Sauvin, if anyone, could bring out its best.

"Go down, Jean, and listen to the tone in the ambulatory," Sauvin said. "We won't worry about disturbing St. Stephen, will we, Pierre?" And they smiled at a private joke.

"Permit me to accompany you," said Pierre. His French was not as deliberate as the old man's but I got him most of the time.

He walked me through the nave which had high rounded arches, talking all the time about the church. It burned long ago and some priest named Stephen got the people to rebuild bigger and better. The Duke of Touraine, from down the river, commissioned many of the windows. He and his Duchess lay in the first chapel, reproduced in cold stone on top of elaborate sarcophagi. Pierre read me the Latin inscriptions. I guess he liked the sound of those old phrases for he walked around both of the tombs in a sober repeat chorus. He pointed out that the Duke had his feet crossed, a sign that he had taken part in a Crusade. I said it might have been better if he had kept his fingers crossed, but when I had to explain I gave up quickly.

Sauvin began to try out the stops. The bass came through better than I expected, echoing through the arches and flowing into the side wings with good resonance.

Pierre proudly showed me the pulpit at the right side of the nave. A more complicated ridiculous affair I have never seen. It looked like a heavily carved sedan chair balanced on the back of a giant Atlas. A row of fat angels blowing horns surrounded its canopy, put there either to cheer Atlas or drown out the sermons -- who knows? Nearby hung a large painting, a Nativity scene. The canvas was cracked in many places but the colors were still strong.

"We do not know the artist," Pierre said, scanning the bottom of the picture as if yet to find a signature. "I requested a man to come from the Louvre to inspect it. He ascribed it to an Italian school of the time of Raphael. Naturally it is not a Raphael, too sombre. Notice the shepherds, the way their feet are wrapped. I ask you, is that Italian of that period? And that poor lamb, lying right in the center. I've never been able to decide whether he is dead or not. I hate to think he is." He inspected the painting from a side angle and shook his head. "Notice the sad expression on Mary's face -- she knows what is ahead."

We stepped out onto a dusty cluttered veranda. Pillars, tops of pillars, and big squares of stone lay here and there on the stone walks. A cloister, I take it, is a place the priests go to get away from it all. For contemplation, Pierre said. I could understand why they might like this one with its walks going toward the river bordered by cypress trees someone had planted years ago. We stood there a minute looking beyond the church to fields of ripe grain, shimmering in a haze of yellow sun. It surely was another world.

Inside again we came face to face with a life-size figure of Jesus hanging on a cross. It gave me quite a jolt; apparently they don't believe in leaving out any of the agonizing details. Pierre opened the offering box below the statue, looked in, shut it. Gently he dusted the pierced feet of Jesus with his handkerchief, shaking his head sadly.

The master was swinging into Bach as we walked up to the altar and his steady powerful notes gave me goose-pimples on my arms. It was true, as Pierre said, this old building really had a voice at last. I waved to Sauvin, but of course he was not looking around. I could see the back of his bald head bobbing in rhythm. Slow, steady, repetitious, he was building with Bach, phrase by phrase, stone by stone.

Six shoulder-high candlesticks guarded the crucifix on the altar. On each side rose dark wooden choir stalls and between them stood a fantastic mahogany lectern. A fierce and ugly carved griffin supported a great shield which became the tilted lectern. It was enough to scare the speech out of anyone.

Noting my surprise Pierre said, "A symbol of vigilance."

"Terrific," I said. "But such an animal, half lion, half eagle, never existed."

"The Word of God should have such power," he remarked, adjusting the angle of the lectern. "I wonder if the Bishop has need of this this afternoon."

Sauvin was trying out the flute stops with a Mozart. The tone came clear, even better than the bass. Pierre smiled as he heard the Mozart.

"Have you heard the organ at the Eglise St.Nazaire in Carcassonne?" he asked. "If I remember, it was one of the first, 1522, in the style of Louis XIII. About 1682 it was overhauled and made the best in the realm by the famous Jean de Joyeuse. A name appropriate, do you not think? At the beginning of this century the organ was restored once more, but alas, they say it needs it now again. How long will our organ perform?"

He beckoned me to follow him around the ambulatory. "These carvings on the choir screen are some of our most precious possessions. This station, Jesus on the Cross, was done by a German who moved here in the reign of Francis I.

I have often thought he might have studied with Dürer. Do you not see a similarity of Dürer's woodcuts of the Passion?"

He hesitated beside a passage leading down to a dark region below. "St. Stephen is there in the crypt, as well as many early unknowns. St. Stephen lost his right hand in the great fire trying to rescue the sacred tunic. The tunic was given to the people of the church by King Pépin in 768. Unfortunately it was destroyed. But pilgrims commenced coming to St. Martin because certain miracles were performed by the touch of St. Stephen's mutilated hand. From as far away as Paris and Rome they came. We were a crossroads for the suffering ones."

Pierre stopped at a cloth-covered figure. "We are repairing the Duke of Roquebrune as well as the walls in this chapel." He removed a sheet to reveal the seated figure of an imperious man who held a script in one hand and a lance in the other. "Even though he is not yet presentable he should be uncovered for the ceremony. I would not want the people to forget the Duke, for it was with his support we finished the second tower and with his gold that we purchased the bells."

It seemed as though bells were ringing, but it was Sauvin pounding away on a Handel. "One more thing I must show you." Pierre touched my arm confidentially. "This little private chapel below the stairs, it is named the Room of St. Stephen. Here the priests come for prayer before they present themselves to the people. It is a place reserved only for the dedicated."

This small chamber was actually the base of the south tower. Two niches, high, narrow and open to the weather, gave it a dim light. On the wall hung an empty rough cross. The stones beneath the cross were worn into a hollow trough. It was a cell -- austere, forbidding, cold. I was relieved when he closed the door.

Monsieur Sauvin came down the stairs talking to himself. I could tell he was satisfied with the workout. I took him to the home of the mayor and went to Suzanne's for my lunch. She served a good plate lunch, veal with mushrooms, generous with the mushrooms. The *vin ordinaire*, red, had a fruity taste. It was local, not Algerian.

To kill time I walked across the river to the little park -- not much, some gravel paths laid out in patterns and a few white urns spilling over with purple and white petunias. It did provide a full side view of St. Martin, which sat on the river bank like a fussy mother hen, its heavy buttresses fluffed out, more or less on guard -- solid, definitely solid.

The shade was cool so I took over a bench under a tree. On the way down from Paris I had asked Sauvin what he was going to play.

"Oh, I sent them a program," he chuckled. "But I won't decide until I get there, try the organ, see the crowd."

"Improvise?" I was afraid he might. He was famous for it. Personally, I think that sort of business is not quite professional. It can be pretty awful.

"No, Jean," he said slowly. He began to work his fingers of his right hand with his left. "I'll play Bach and more Bach. Perhaps Buxtehude, his E Minor Prelude and Fugue. Palestrina, one of his masses. Palestrina is so ancient he is in tune with today. He's far out, as you say, all free flowing, no bars in his music. Yes, the early ones belong to St Martin."

"No moderns?" I knew he could.

"One, perhaps Messiaen. We must bring them through to today. And of course I will play the "Ave Maria" for my mother and because all who are mothers or who have mothers will then be happy. But naturally, most of the itme I'll be giving them Sauvin."

"When I play I aim for as true an interpretation as is possible," I said rather emphatically. I prided myself on my scholarship in that area.

"What is music?" he asked me then, clapping his hands in time to the motor. I did not answer. After all, I am not a beginner.

With eyes on the countryside he went on, "Music is a voice. It says something. Today I play for the people of St. Martin-du-Bois. I know them. For a thousand years they have been building their church. There they have been baptized, married, and finally interred. It is still unfinished. Today I think I shall finish it for them. I'll make for them a beautiful place, more beautiful than they have ever dreamed. It will not last a thousand ycars -- ten minutes,

maybe. But once they see it they will be filled
with such longing they will never be the same
again."

"Monsieur Sauvin," I said, "what people
imagine when I play is not in my power. Music
has always gone beyond the representational
into the abstract. Let the listeners struggle
along; most of them do not understand anyway.

"Pardon me." He jerked his head and
stared at me. "Jean, your technique is excellent,
your footwork is better than mine at your age.
But as you know, technique is only the beginning, music comes after. Music is a voice; it tells
of suffering, joy, glory. The dedicated artist
speaks for more than himself -- maybe for all
civilization. This you do not fully understand;
some never do. Yes, I think today I shall speak
for all who have built this church -- from the
beginning -- and I shall take them, my friends of
the village, through their agony to that final
heavenly place, the beauty they have not yet
reached, the place we see only far, far in the
distance, only hear echoes . . . "

He shut his eyes and put his head back
and remained quiet until we reached his village.

The Duke of Roquebrune's bells rang out
that afternoon until all comers were in church,
seated on chairs in the nave or standing in the
wings. The ceremony of dedication had dignity,
even drama, though I saw no reason for the
mayor to read the hundred and fifty names of
donors, names printed already on the program.
Then he, fearing he had left someone out, asked
that all who had contributed in some way stand.

People began to stand, slowly, until like a moving carpet the whole congregtion was on its feet. Unconsciously I stood with them, guilty when I realized what I was doing. But after all, I did drive Sauvin down. The choir from Touraine was more than acceptable, the voices of the boys stayed in pitch in the echoing vaults. The Bishop, handsome in his mitre and red robes, blessed the organ, the church it served, the souls of those whose effort built this church, and all the press of human beings within the reach of his voice. Tapers flickered in the chapels and the six great candles blazed at the altar. Above us the great stone arches loomed as if they were there for another thousand years. The light from the high west stained-glass windows flowed in on strips of red and blue and golden dust upon us all.

Then it was Sauvin's turn to play. He led us steadily along from Palestrina and Buxtehude, through Bach and Handel, up to today. Of course, he stayed longest with Bach. I suppose the fugues were lost on most of the audience, yet I'm sure Sauvin felt them essential. I began to sense that he was doing the concert for the organ itself -- fearing no one else would ever give it a chance to demonstrate its full power. Then I suspected it was Sauvin himself he was giving us -- Sauvin from baptism in one of the side chapels to Sauvin today, riding up there in control. He got it all in -- adventure, agony, struggle. He ended with a powerful chord that was a wild statement of confidence. The tones filled to bursting every cubic inch of the church

and every transfixed soul within it. It was a
tremendous performance. I said to myself, if
nothing else happens all summer, this is it.

Then the Bishop, the attending priests,
the mayor, the officials and all the people filed
out while Sauvin meandered away at a
recessional. The big doors stood open and a
warm breeze made the candles sputter and
dance. I waited in back for Sauvin to come
down. Pierre too was still there, leaning against
one of the columns. If we left soon we might
make Paris by dark.

But Sauvin was not stopping; he started
to improvise. People outside, shaking hands and
laughing, heard the music and did not go away.
I wondered what had come over the man. The
organ swelled and throbbed until it caught up
my own heartbeat and magnified it a thousand
times. I thought my heart would jump out of my
chest. Dizzily I sat down. Could it be the mushrooms? No, hardly.

I recognized a part of Handel's *Messiah*, á
la Sauvin. It roared from chord to chord and I
found myself struggling, drowning in it. The
man was reckless beyond all technique, he was
delirious, intoxicated with sound. Then I noticed
the music was affecting other things too. The
supporting arches seemed to recede and the air
was filled with a pulsing like sunlight under
water. In the chapel I thought I saw the Duke of
Touraine stir on top of his long cold sarcopha-
gus and reach his arm across to the Duchess
who turned slightly at his touch. I saw movement in the nave. Atlas shifted the heavy pulpit

on his shoulders and the angels on its canopy
flew up like doves and began to blow their
horns. It sounded like Mozart, no, it was Sauvin
on the trompette. Angel horns everywhere. They
filled the nave with a delicate rising crescendo
ushering us, no, welcoming us, no, announcing
us as we stood at the gates of a heavenly city.

After the angel horns came "Jesu Joy of
Man's Desiring." Sauvin hid it in a fugue but it
was unmistakable. Candle smoke and incense
swirled like fog across the front of the church.
The figure of Jesus on the Cross swirled too.
Jesus raised his head with the dried blood and
the crown of thorns and cried out loudly,
"Father, Father." I heard his plea. In the Nativity
painting Mary seemed to smile at her new baby;
she was not sad. And the lamb -- its tail moved,
it tried to stand up, it did stand up! Pierre,
Pierre, do you see?

The organ began to hammer, jumping in
rhythmic taps. It could be men in white aprons
hammering and chiselling around the choir
stalls. To add to the confusion a loud voice
began to speak from somewhere behind the
choir, "Rise up, go forth." There in the distance
was St. Stephen with both arms raised, one his
stump, addressing a mass of pilgrims crowded
together on the steps of the crypt. His hair blew
in the wind, the wind which was making all the
candles flicker and was sweeping the sun's last
yellow rays into streamers across the altar. The
griffin holding the lectern spread his wings out
into a great arc and added a piercing, unearthly
screech.

Then the music slowed. I recognized parts of "Before Thy Throne I Stand" from the blind and dying Bach. Then Sauvin picked up again more wildly, crashing from chord to chord without transition, pounding like breakers on a beach. I had to get out. The church was moving; it was heaving and throbbing. St. Martin was a live thing. It was not stone arches, mouldy foundations, iron-braced doors -- it was bleeding and sweating and crying in anguish.

I choked with a strange sorrow, my chest smoldered fire. I moved back to escape. Hundreds of people stood in the square, faces turned toward the doors from which poured the tumult of sound. Unready to face them, I opened the narrow door to the Room of St. Stephen. The room of the dedicated welcomed me. It was cold, quiet, and magnificently bare. I stood there, kneading my hands, until the music stopped.

When I heard Sauvin's shuffle on the stairs I went out. He was smiling a drained-out, happy smile. I started to speak but words were nothing. Maybe my music some day would say it.

About the Last Three Stories

Two of the following stories come obviously out of our years in Washington, D.C. "The Island" grew from a trip we once took on the Adriatic. Unlike Angela, I was a happy and willing traveler. The Island I now own has no sea wall of rocks covered with Oleander vines. It is fortified instead by a wall of books that tell the history of mankind. My view is of gentle rolling hills, green trees, and the ever changing sky. There is a distant hum of traffic which competes with more welcome bird song. On summer evenings I walk to my tiny garden and gather fragrant roses.

Welcome to my island where I relive my memories and contemplate our amazing world.

The Island

I first saw him at the pier in Venice as we were waiting to board ship for Dubrovnik. Chance does change one's life.

Our Jadrolinija travel folder read, "Boarding at nine. Sailing at eleven." Our ship loomed white and silent at the dock, its gangplank tilting at a precarious angle and a giant gap in its side waiting for loading. The station was an empty yawning cavern with faint noises of activity in the rear. A light snapped on above a bar pointing up a coffee machine, bottles and a man in a black apron. We ordered expresso and carried our cups to a wobbly iron table.

"This *is* sea travel," Burt remarked. "You'll like it."

After a jet from New York this was a change, though I was not sure I liked it. It only prolonged our trip. I was tired of travel, of crowds and strangeness. I was tired of -- well, I was tired. But Italians do know how to make coffee. Over my cup I noted the passengers as they arrived, with their raincoats, their cameras, their bulky suitcases and their worried expressions. A group of English men and women, five in all, an American family, a middle-aged American couple, three, four Germans, or they could be Dutch, then several Serbs -- or were they Croatians?-- not many, but still enough to contain one or two who could be of interest. The newcomers milled around, lining up by the customs wicket, or just sitting and staring like we did.

One gets talked out in travelling. Burt and I actually don't talk much anyway. Trivia has become so trivial and important things too important to explore. I wandered over to a window. After all, it was still Venice out there. At that moment a launch pulled up in a wash of waves. A tall man climbed on to the dock; someone handed hm a violin case; porters closed in on his baggage. Then the launch roared off again, full throttle, its flags almost torn off in the speed. As the man walked toward the station the wind blew his grey-black hair up in a ruff. His black trench coat fit as close as an iris leaf. His face -- I stared. Rachmaninoff is dead. Yet here was the same world-weary sardonic expression, the same long sad elegant features of the face on my girlhood record albums. Only this man carried a violin.

Burt called to me just then. The customs man had opened his wicket and it was time to go aboard. We had difficulty locating our cabin. Evans is a simple name, but apparently it doesn't look the same to Yugoslavians.

Our cabin, when we did get it, was narrow and a little dirty around the edges. There were bunk beds, a hard green settee with a broken cushion, a scratched up desk, also white towels and soap in the bathroom and a dripping shower that couldn't be shut completely off. We unpacked systematically. Burt has taught me to do this and is always upset if I don't. When we felt the ship moving we hurried up on deck to say a last goodbye to Venice.

"She's a glittering merchant," Burt said.

"And to think it all began with the selling of salt."

"No other city in the world like it," I repeated the guide books. "St. Marks, the pigeons, the gondoliers, the Grand Canal. But what I'll remember longest is that little island we passed on our way in from the airport. Do you remember how it sat so contentedly in the sun, the villa a faded Venetian red with white pillars, grape vines on a trellis? Remember the boat ramp guarded by a couple of old chipped-up Greek statues?"

Burt nodded, "But who wants to live on an island, cut off from everything?"

"I wish we had a place of our own, Burt. It wouldn't cost much more than our New York apartment, would it? If we were settled down, rooted, maybe I'd feel -- oh, organized."

He didn't say anything. I went on anyway. "I don't mean you should change your work. You wouldn't do that, I know."

He grunted and got out his pipe. Lights from the mansions along the canal ran out to us in silver streamers. Our ship moved steadily away -- away from the leaning candystripe water poles, away from the gay hotel terraces with their red tablecloths, away from the swan-like gliding gondolas. We had one last glimpse of the shimmering Maria della Salute, the lacy arches of the Doge Palace, the towering Campanile before they too faded. With a numb indifference I let them return to the old paintings of Whistler and Turner, where for me they had always resided.

"Let's go up top, Angie, and watch the
pilot leave," Burt suggested. The wind came at
us on the upper deck and I was glad for my
cashmere coat. I tied my new Italian scarf twice
around my head.

"Where is the North Star?" I asked to get
my bearings. As if a star could in any way put
me on course. Yet, Polaris was at least one
familiar friend in our wanderings.

The lights grew more distant. The moonlight took over. "I feel my Viking ancestors
stirring," I said facing into the wind. Burt was
amused. I'd forgotten the excitement, the
mystery of a ship's departure, the quiet but in-
exorable take-off into the unknown. I breathed
deeply the sea air.

The captain came out and spoke to us in
slow English, "You like ship travel?"

"My wife didn't want to come," Burt said.
"But now she is beginning to be pleased."

"September is good," the captain said.
"Too hot with the engines in summer."

He saluted a tall person near us, speaking
to him in Italian. It was the man who had come
in the fast launch. He was pointing to an island
we were approaching. A floodlight on a dock
lighted up a massive rock wall softened a little
by overhanging oleander bushes. The captain
stepped back into his quarters and we heard a
sharp blast of the horn.

"My island," the tall man said to Burt.
"They signal my farewell." His voice was clear,
his English formal, he even smiled a little.

Burt nodded. I fixed my eyes on the red

oleander blossoms that tumbled from the ramparts of the island, but like the red table-cloths of the Europa Hotel they too were disappearing. We stood silently at the rail, moving together over the ancient Adriatic, staring for altogether different reasons at one tiny spot of earth. And the dock light blinked in recognition of our passing.

Then the wind increased. It whipped my scarf out into a long streamer to match the black billows of smoke that were pouring from the smokestack. The engines began a faster steadier throbbing, indicating the course was set. We went below and, without further talk, to bed.

The sun spotlighted through the porthole in the morning and woke us. We heard a clanging and bumping on deck and felt a reduction in speed. Burt climbed down from the upper berth to peer out.

"We're coming into a harbor, a good sized city. Must be Rijeka, old Fiume. A rugged coast! Water is really blue, cobalt blue, just as they say. Get up, we've got to see it. There's a seven or eight hour layover." He stretched his big frame and easily touched the ceiling.

"I'm going to stay right here and rest," I said. "You don't know anyone here do you?"

"No, but I think Josep at the Yugoslavian desk of the U.N. is from here. Maybe I can learn something about the Yugoslavs. After all, that's part of my job."

"But this is our vacation; or is it? I wish

we had gone to the Poconos where it is safe and restful. But no, we have to go to Dubrovnik, then to Athens, maybe Crete -- who knows where -- to find a man who knows the man who is the man . . ."

"But he was with Hammarskjold five years ago, the day before the flight to the Congo. This man, as I've said a hundred times, was going but changed his mind. He must know something."

"What if he does? It won't bring Dag Hammarskjold back."

Burt assumed his overly patient look. He wasn't exactly at his best, needed a shave as well as a haircut. But when he dropped off his pajamas his muscles, which always surprised me, made up for his scowl.

"Angela," I prepared myself for a lecture. "Hammarskjold was my boss. You know how I feel about him. Besides, when in Athens I can work on that UNESCO problem and justify my time at least. If I can only locate that man -- I saw him once years ago -- we might know once and for all if it were an accident."

I turned my head away. Yes, I had heard it before, many times. Burt was Burt. I couldn't change him if I wanted to. But myself -- did I want to go along like this forever? "I wish we could live normal lives," I said to the wall. "A house, a neighborhood, roots, yes, even P.T.A. and Women's Clubs. Instead we are mixed up with everybody's lives, all around the world it seems, situations unpredictable, even dangerous. I wish you were a gas station operator (I didn't, really). At least then life would be simple."

Burt went into the shower, leaving me stranded. What use is sun shining on the blue Adriatic when life is muddy and wretched? I remember the doctor saying, 'If you wouldn't tense up so, Mrs. Evans, about things you can't do anything about, you'd have no difficulty in conceiving.' Well, Burt wants children too.

"If we ever have a boy or girl," I said sitting up when Burt came back in, "we'd have to settle down and establish roots."

"My children won't lack roots," he said pulling on his shorts and beginning his arm exercises. There was not room to swing his arms so he started on his kneebends. "My children will know the world, know it for what it is -- a great big houseful of nincompoops. Still, it is our world." He stopped to inhale deeply. "If my son wants to run a gas station, O.K. I don't. This is a new age. I'm part of it. Could be a better world, but someone has to make the effort." He began to count the deep kneebends.

I got up, of course I always follow along, and we set out. I warmed up as we went. Exploring a city is a science with Burt. Very little escapes his attention. Rijeka stretches along the shore like an animated map pinned against bleached out rocky hills. The ruins of a castle top a high point. We went in and out of stores, magazine shops, bakeries, the outdoor market, even the city library where we looked up names of American books in the card catalog. Near noon, on our way back to the boat, we

stopped at a sidewalk cafe for *cafe au lait*. The
shade of the awning was welcome. Petunias
blooming in boxes reminded me of home.

"One orders Turkish coffee here," said a
man at the next table, putting down his Italian
newspaper. It was the Signor we had talked to
last night. "Have you been to the castle?"

"Perhaps this afternoon," Burt said. "Is it
worth the trip?"

"An excellent view," the man said. "I can
obtain a car. Would you accompany me? The
ship departs at five, we could go up at three."

"We prefer the tram," Burt said rather
shortly. Then seeing the man's face stiffen, he
quickly added, "Take the tram with us, it's
always a better way to get acquaintd with the
people."

So, later that afternoon we climbed with
the Signor to the castle tower. It gave a complete
view of the harbor. The streets below us were
crawling with little cement-colored cars, stubby
brown trams, and flocks of people. Burt pointed
out our ship taking on cargo. Behind us the
barren mountain sloped steeply down into a
forbidding gully. Hills, more hills, flowed one
into the other inland from the sea. Eroded,
devastated, as white as old bones! I was in
accord with their wild desolation and turned my
back to the busy harbor. I felt strangely cousin
to a straggling dusty vine that clung to the base
of the tower, not doing very well in the gravel
but clinging.

"The men who built here took advantage
of both harbor and mountain," Burt pointed out.

"See, they used native rock."

"It's all a ruin now," I said. "Not even much of a museum."

"Come," said the Signor. "They serve beer on the terrace. One must take pleasure in what remains."

We found a table on the shady side of the terrace. "Are you stopping at Dubrovnik?" Burt asked.

"Yes, I give two concerts there, in the Rector's Palace -- an ancient and beautiful place to play." He beckoned to a waiter and ordered beer in German. I tried to recall names of violinists.

"What will you play?" I asked.

"All Paganinni one evening. With the Symphony it will be Brahms."

"I heard Fransescotti once in Washington," I offered. "It was a peak in my life."

The Signor hunted in his coat pocket and handed me a printed program.

"Sergie Antonovich," I read aloud. "We are honored to be with you."

He shrugged his shoulders and flexed his long fingers. "I play well. I should. It is my life work -- to produce the sound, sad, happy, whatever is required. But after my work comes my island; you saw it as we left Venice. There I build the most beautiful place in the world. Everything is the best -- I collect in my travels. Even the soil I bring. But now, Tania has gone, and I am depressed."

"Your wife?" I made a sympathetic sound.

He nodded, gazing over the terrace wall at

144

the city below. The beer was not very cold.
Surprisingly warm day, for September.

The silence became long. I remarked, "It
must be wonderful to have a place like yours. I
remember the rock wall and the oleander
bushes, but we couldn't see what it was really
like."

"It's my second skin," he patted his long
sallow cheek. "I change, but my house and my
island, unlike me, they grow more beautiful
each year."

"Do you have a vineyard?" I asked. Burt
was paying little attention to our conversation.

"Of course. I have a vineyard, a fountain,
even a Bellini on the wall, Gentile, not Jacopo.
My wine is like the Dalmatian wines, very
robust. Tonight, if you will permit me to sit at
your table, I'll order some wine like it. You can
then judge its excellence."

"Why not?" Burt said, draining his beer
glass and standing up. "We'd better start back to
the ship."

Shortly before the ship sailed three
busloads of young people, obviously students,
came up the gangplank carrying German rück-
sacks, Sears Roebuck sleeping bags, transistor
radios, watermelons, all sorts of gear. A cheer
went up for the last fellow, fat and red-bearded,
who came running with an immense wicker-
covered wine bottle on his back. I expected a
noisy trip from then on, but most of them filed
past us to the upper deck and left us alone. Two
students, American in appearance, she
especially appealing with a pixie haircut so

different from the usual long stringy locks,
carried cushions to the prow of our deck and
settled down out of the wind. When the crew
pulled up anchor one sailor stepped over to
them. There was a slight argument, with gest-
ures. They picked up their cushions and went
up the stairs.

"They're allowed to sleep on the upper
deck," said Burt. "Students love Yugoslavia --
it's still cheap. I'm going up and talk with them.
See what I can find out."

I went below to shower and change before
dinner. I shook out my best blue silk -- not too
wrinkled. It matched my eyes, Burt always said.
A lighter blue than the Adriatic which sparkled
like sapphires through the porthole and threw
flickers of light into the cabin. I was teasing my
top hair into a puff when Burt came in.

"Hmmm! Prefume! Why the finery? You're
too good looking as it is. Just a dizzy blonde, the
boys fall down in rows, even Sergie the fiddler. I
saw the way he inspected your peacherino skin,
your legs. He didn't miss a thing."

"Don't be absurd." It was an outrage to be
spoken to like an object up for auction. "Maybe
he appreciates the finer things -- not just
measurements either."

Burt stepped around me and plopped on
the settee. My hair never will go up right when
he is watching me, but there wasn't room for
both of us to dress at once.

"I can see his villa," Burt went on. "Thick
oriental rugs, pictures in heavy gilt frames (no
doubt a light on the Bellini), wine glasses from

Murano, petrified artiness so thick it gags. Villa Tatti and Berenson -- brought up to date. Is that what you want for us? Is that what you go for?"

I tried to stay calm, objective. "He's not a dilettante, he's a performing artist. He's reached a peak in his art. That means something, doesn't it? And what's more, he has built himself a beautiful little world. A place just exactly as he wants it. I'm beginning to think (I was beginning to preach -- which gets me nowhere with Burt) perhaps the greatest art is to control one's own life. What are we making of ours? Things and places always shifting; always new problems; nothing to hold on to." I grabbed a towel to cover my face. We would go from dis-integration to gradual dissolution, and finally numbness. I could not stand it. My makeup all on too. Why couldn't I stay calm?

"Take it easy, Angie," Burt walked around me to the bathroom. "If you don't see what we have to hold on to it is probably not there for you. Maybe it never will be if you have to have all the paraphernalia, the trappings of life first. I don't give a damn if my life is a work of art. My life is useful, that's what is important. People, not things, are what count. Do you think I care whether my bed is Louis Quinze if you are in it?"

I couldn't answer. My throat was stopped and I was pressing hard on my eyes to keep the tears back.

"Which reminds me," he went on, throw-ing his clothes on the settee, piece by piece from the bathroom. "That young couple, remember them on the deck? From Michigan State, Peace Corps. going back to Turkey after a vacation in Austria. Nice kids. She's not well. More than seasick. I gave her all my Xamamina tablets. You still have some, don't you?"

I nodded, keeping the towel over my face.

Sergie Antonovich ate dinner with us, sitting at the head of the table next to me. The wine he ordered was like a Riesling whose grapes by good fortune had enjoyed a Mediterranean summer. He was right -- it was superb. Burt and the middle-aged American couple (from Virginia, we discovered) sat across from me. An Englishman and his attractive wife were on my side of the table. Until tonight the Englishman's wife had appeared in slacks and a bulky turtle-neck sweater. Now, in soft print, neck perhaps a little low, she was glamorous.

"Salute," Sregie Antonovich said, raising his glass.

"Prosit," said the woman beside me. So, she was actaully German. "We're going to Hvar," she added. "Hvar is wundershöen. A big island, much white sand, a small hotel, good food. We found it by accident last year and are going back now for two weeks."

"A great place," said her husband, hunched over his soup. "They leave you alone, quite alone, you know. It's a big island, lots of room."

The man from Virginia got out his boat schedule, "I see we put in there about noon tomorrow." He smiled a corn cob smile at his wife who nodded but said nothing.

"The grapes in my vineyard are full and heavy this summer," said Signor Antonovich, turning his wine glass in his long fingers. "It could be a vintage year. Perhaps you and Signor Evans would visit me on your return from Athens. I am there until November, then New York and San Francisco. You Americans love music, Signora, and you pay well for it."

"We appreciate the best though we do not always produce it," I said. "But give us a few more generations. Even now, look at our bridges, our skyscrapers, our Lincoln Center. . ."

"And the great American girl," Burt interrupted leering slightly, but definitely leering at me. "Seriously, Signor Antonovich, the United States still has resources, energy, and even hope -- a good combination in one package. We may blunder, but we still try."

"Resources and energy," repeated the Englishman. "You are right there. But as to hope -- you have a way of dashing that out for some of us. I'd say the world situation is more precarious and less hopeful today than it was ten years ago."

"And so," Signor Antonovich raised his glass, "One lives but a few years. I make an island in this world -- a fortress from the storms. With my own hands I build it. When comes the time people no longer ask for my music, then I play to the fishes. Salute!"

"How right you are," the Virginian raised his glass to his wife's.

Burt was scowling but said nothing. Dinner, which had begun with gaiety and camaraderie, seemed to be petering out. Everyone was crawling back into his own hole. But what was the great expectation? I, I guess, was the foolish one. I should know better than to keep on looking for revelations from odd assortments of people.

After dinner we took a turn around the deck and saw the young man from Michigan talking to one of the cooks at the door of the galley. "Oh, Mr. Evans," he called. "Maybe you can help me. I have no Serbian and my German is anything but fluent. I want a lemon for Betty, some tea, anything hot. I'm not getting through."

"Sure, Mike," Burt said, introducing us. At that moment our dining room steward appeared and Burt talked to him in German. Soon the steward handed Burt a bowl of soup covered with a white napkin.

"Lead the way," Burt said as we climbed to the top deck. Students were settling into deck chairs and benches for the night. One young man was tending a portable phonograph on the counter of the bar. Somewhere a guitar was being strummed. Betty, in semi-private quarters behind a long wooden bench, lay on a coat and two cushions.

"The best we can do," Mike explained to me in a low voice. "She needs to be near the W.C. I wish I could go in with her to hold her head when she is sick."

I winced, remembering the odor of the
public lavatories we passed on the deck.

"I suppose she could . . .," and then I
stopped. No. Why give up our cabin, reserved so
long in advance? Burt was looking at me appealingly. The first time I encountered that look was
on our honeymoon, and two Hungarian refugees
came home and stayed with us four weeks. The
next time it was Raoul, the Cuban, then Roaul's
wife, then his sister. There was the Nigerian boy
for whom Burt got a scholarship at Columbia,
and (how could I forget her) the cousin of the
Swedish representative to the U.N.

I looked out over the water which was not
sparkling blue but black and opaque in the
night. All those people had used us, then they
went on their way leaving us with grocery bills,
dirty laundry, long distance telephone bills,
headaches from trying to solve their problems.
'Our home is your home,' Burt always said,
opening his arms wide. A four room apartment!
Why was I resentful? I honestly felt sorry for
those people. What I resented I suppose was
being buffeted around by everyone when our
own life together needed something more solid,
a core. I'm not ready to embrace the world -- if I
did it would tear me into a hundred pieces.

But Burt was smiling his big open childish smile, looking as young as Mike, his blond
hair falling over one eye. I nodded assent.

Burt put the soup carefully on the deck
beside Betty. "Look here Mike, let's take this
young lady down to our cabin and put her on
the lower bunk. The bathroom is only a step

away. Angie can sleep above and you and I can take turns on the settee."

So that is what we did, except after settling Betty I insisted on Burt sleeping first shift. I never drop off easily. With a *Guide to Yugoslavia* under my arm I went up to the lounge and hunted a comfortable wicker chair. Betty could be pregnant, she had no fever. The kids were worried. What about their Peace Corps jobs? Could she go back to Michigan? Well, that was one thing I couldn't do anything about. I opened the book to *Split* where we would be stopping in the morning.

The Englishman and his Brunhilda came in and beckoned me to join them at a table. "We're having Istra Bitters -- try some."

It turned out to be a pink drink, bitter and pleasing.

"Why don't you stop off at Hvar?" the man suggested. "Islands are great for vacations. They isolate you yet they themselves are always encompassing."

"Encompassing, that's what I wanted. A place to know from shore to shore, boundaries that were definite. "I'd love it, but we can't."

"Business?" she asked.

"Yes," I said.

I went out on deck. The moon was up, looking a little silly as it leaned over backward, being past the full. I took cover from the wind on the leeward side and walked back and forth to keep warm. A figure in a black trench coat came around the corner and we met. It was Sergie Antonovich. He stopped beside me and leaned on the rail. The water below made a soft insistent swish as the ship cut its way forward. The Dalmatian coast presented a dark jagged pattern on the horizon.

"Will you come to hear me in Dubrovnik?" he asked.

"Unfortunately we must go on before your concert. I regret this very much."

He sighed and buttoned up the collar of his coat more tightly. "I too regret. Your presence would inspire my best. An artist speaks most truly in his art. Maybe you and your husband will come back to Venice and will stop at my island."

"I would love to come, but Burt must stay a while in Athens. Then we fly back to New York."

His eyes were dark holes. His face in the moonlight was uneven, wavering with the uncertain lines of an El Greco saint. Whatever was smoldering would ignite with the slightest spark.

"If Signor Evans could not spare the time maybe you could stop a few days as he goes about his business. Don't draw back Signora; I have a housekeeper, a gardener, others. It is as they say in your country, 'on the up and up'. I simply offer."

Not daring to look at him I studied the stars. The constellations were not the same as those at home. These were the ones consulted by the early Greek mariners as they set out in exploration, in adventure.

"Signor," I turned to go back in. "Thank

153

you. No doubt your island would be a glimpse of paradise. I will speak to my husband."

Burt was in the lounge looking for me. "Go down and get some sleep," he ordered. "I'll come down in a couple hours when Mike shifts with me. Betty seems to be quiet."

I mentioned Signor Antonovich and his invitation to us.

"What?" he stared at me. "That old so-and-so! Were you taken in? Well, if you really want to go, go ahead, just go. But you'll have a long long wait before I'd come by and pick you up."

I put up my chin. "You don't understand. It's the island -- so perfect -- so beautiful. Burt, why can't we find a place to settle down? Must we always be wanderers!"

"Angela, I'm not a wanderer. I'm a member of the human race. I want to be used. If I wanted to sit on a rock, play siren music, bury myself under *objects d'art* I would not be me. There isn't time for both. I've made my choice. What about you?"

I kept my chin up until I got to the stairs, then it began to quiver. By the time I reached the stateroom I could hold it steadier.

As we steamed into Dubrovnik I could see Signor Antonovich seeking me out. I had avoided him all day, spending most of my time with Betty. I even skipped lunch. Now, all the luggage was stacked in rows on the deck. We had our coats and purses in hand. All was in readiness for debarking.

I moved back to where Signor Antonovich was standing. He said nothing, looking down at me with polite attention.

"Goodbye, signor Antonovich," I held out my hand. "I am grateful to you. I shall many times dream of your island, but I begin now to build my own. I start from within."

With the courtly style of the old world, he bent and kissed my hand.

D X 235

The chocolate cake is in the oven and the timer set. After all that happened this past week baking a cake is a welcome relaxation. No one could have predicted what I've been through, and all in the line of duty, so to speak.

Last fall I took a part time job doing bibliographical work. This means I go to the Library of Congress two or three times a week to check book lists. I really enjoy the work because I get out of the house and see all kinds of people. I am, without apologies, a typical suburban housewife, given to wearing a navy blue tweed suit (a very good one now in its sixth year), crisp white blouses (starched, not drip-dry), and honest walking shoes. My husband and I still take walks in the evening. I wear glasses when I read and this so recently that I even enjoy the little preliminary involved in putting them on. Strangers often speak to me, and in spite of warnings by my husband, I usually answer. I'll never forget the time in Paris, along the Champs de Mars, when some tourists asked me the way to the Eiffel Tower. But I am getting off my subject.

To continue with my *Who's Who*. We live in Washington, D.C. where people seem to expect the dramatic and the unexplicable to happen. And it does. And to think that I, I who never wear a sari or a belted English coat and never go to first nights or Her Majesty's birthday parties, should become involved in the affairs of the . . .Well, there are certain agencies one does not mention, so I cannot divulge all the details. But I hasten to assure you that I am a loyal though often puzzled American citizen, without amendments.

Everyone who knows Washington has seen the Library of Congress, that fat dowager of a building in a green copper hat sitting deter-minedly behind the Capitol and backed up by an austerely modern Annex on Second Street. If the variation in architecture disturbs you re-member that your teen-aged daughter is probably streamlined too. Our project has a study room in the Annex, up on the fifth floor where there is a wonderful view of the city. We are lucky, air-conditioned you know, while the old building has only fans.

I'm not a scholar, only a taker-care-of scholars. I've lived around them so long that I have much their same coloring. Every morning that I enter the heavy glass revolving door of the Annex I step into their world. Peacefulness engulfs me, inquiry and research quicken me, and a long day of free-wheeling infinite possibili-ties stretches ahead. I marvel at the beauty of the marble halls and the carved brass doors of the quiet elevators, at the formality and helpful-ness of its guards. Like an old firehorse I get excited by the smell, not of smoke of course, but by the distinct indefinable musty, gluey smell of old books, lots and lots of books, dusty piled-up books, leather and paperbacks, folios and bound magazines, and on and on. At times when I stand in the center I feel their weight, tons and tons, like a great protective shell between me and the chaotic outside. Some people may think of this library as a mausoleum, stacked rows of dead, but it is really a collection of voices, each one saying his special piece. You can see why it is exciting to work there, such potential -- and also a degree of protection.

Our study room is at the end of a long corridor of rooms used by an imposing list of scholars, senators, and officials. The name plate on the room next to ours has always been blank and the shade over the glass door pulled two-thirds down. I never managed to drop anything right there in order to peer under. I did notice a short grey-haired hurried man entering or leaving the place a few times but I was usually too far down the hall to speak. But I didn't need to speak to people -- even when spoken to. In fact, I rejoiced in my anonymity and floated free as a ghost, enjoying the remarkable people, puzzling over the strange languages I heard, and listening to scraps of stories told in bitterness or surprise in the elevators or cafeteria.

And so my job at the Library seemed a wonderful adventure until one day last week, Tuesday morning to be exact. I was in the stacks, Deck 2, searching for a book in English history. The checking was going fast, problems were few. I ran my eye along the shelf -- DC 215, DC 230, DC 234. Then came a wrong number. I put my glasses on to be sure. DX 235. An easy mistake to make, DX instead of DC. I pulled the book and looked at it -- Greek history. A nice book in the hand, old, soft binding. I would file it in its right place. No, they prefer that attendants do the shelving. I would put it out on the filing cart as my good turn for the day. The book fell open in my hand and a folded paper dropped out. I slipped the paper back in and then, curious, took it out again. It was not part of that book, it was thin, transparent paper, obviously different. I unfolded it. It was a map carefully drawn by hand, Asia Minor. There were many small words in strange writing, a few German words, several lines drawn between cities or circled spots, numbers like road map numbers on the lines. I couldn't make it out. Someone must have left it in the book by mistake. I glanced at my watch, it was almost noon. I closed my folder and hurried for the elevator, leaving the book on the shelving cart as I went out.

The top stop of the stack elevator lets one out into the Thomas Jefferson Reading Room behind the desk, so I stopped to tell Mr. Burchfield, the desk man, of my discovery. It made me happy to be able to return with even a small service his many kindnesses to me.

"What did you say was the number?" he asked, going through a box of slips on the desk in front of him.

"DX 235."

"That's it all right! That book has been requested every day for a week by a V.I.P. We have only one copy. I've sent out a 'special search' for it. Now thanks to you I'll have it sent right up."

"It had a map in it that was not . . . .," I started to explain. But he was on the telephone calling the stack deck, so I went on.

The narrow low hall to our study room was not the usual quiet corridor where my heels always seemed to make unnecessarily loud click clacks. Today several people were standing at the far end. As I went forward two men came by with a stretcher, a covered figure on it. Next came Rice Bailey, the black man who is our hall attendant. He was breathing loudly, "M-m-mister Sch-Schmidt," he said to me. "He is dead."

"What happened?"

"He m-m-must have been in there all night. I f-f-found him. I-I-I went in there to leave a b-book and f-found him." He was shaking, sweating, and his stuttering was unusual.

"Do you mean the man in the room next to us?"

"Yes. The Lord have mercy on him. He was lying like this, over his desk. But d-d-dead. I touched him, out cold. Been in there all night, maybe. M-m-murder; could be." His eyes rolled up.

"No one would murder a harmless scholar," I said trying to assure us both.

"Sh-sh-Schmidt, M-m-mister Schmidt was w-w-working for a secret agency. D-d-didn't you know? The good Lord has his *own* plans, no one can go against them. His ways are beyond understanding."

As I passed I tried to avoid the people in the hall by not looking at them, but a young man stepped over to me.

"I understand you use this next room. I am Detective Whitelock, Sidmore Whitelock," and he flashed out a leather folder with his credentials. "Could I talk to you? I would like to ask you a few questions."

We stood in Mr. Schmidt's door and I could now see the study room which had always been hidden behind the curtain. It was like all the others, big flat green metal desk, a rolling chair, a metal bookcase, two metal filing cabinets, books, stacks of notes. A man's top coat hung on the upright coat rack and an old brown felt hat tipped across the top hook. Mr. Whitelock stepped just inside, touching nothing, but looking at the row of books across the back of the desk.

"Hmmmm, *The Classical Tradition, The Classical Dictionary,* books might be a clue, certainly a clue to his interest. Did you know Mr. Schmidt very well?"

"No, I hardly ever saw him. I haven't been around the Library very long."

"Any evidence, no matter how small, would be of help."

"You think he was murdered?"

"Cannot say at this point. No violence. But anyone in his work would be a likely target."

I looked past Mr. Whitelock out of the window. The noon sun shone warmly, even gayly upon the dome of the Mother Library across the street and upon the clean white tip of Washington's Monument beyond it. From across the Potomac a giant airplane moved majestically up and across the sky while another circled in for landing. Turning to leave I brushed against the top coat, a tan one like my husband had worn in the army. It hung carelessly, from one shoulder, the wire coat hanger unused on the floor. What had been this man's real work? Where had been his home, his real home? Home is the place we park our hats, someone once said. A study room could be a home. His notes were sorted neatly in several piles on one side of the desk. Some yellow book requests were beside them. I could see, and I looked twice to be sure, the call number on the top slip was DX 235.

"Sorry, I can't help. Terrible, inexplicable, isn't it?" I found I was crying as I went out and into our own study room. As I put my papers in my desk I remembered the map. It was there with my book lists in the manilla folder. I took it out and put it on the bottom of the drawer under everything else and locked the desk before going out to lunch.

I could not get to sleep that night. Poor Mr. Schmidt! Was he a spy? A counterspy? A special agent? What was his secret? He had been born in Vienna, or Budapest -- somewhere over there I recall hearing. What about the book DX 235? Why had he requested it? The map might have been his. If I only had a sample of his writing to compare. When I finally fell asleep I dreamed of a body on a stretcher floating down a long hall toward me. When it passed the body sat up and pointed at me. It was Mr. Whitelock, Mr. Sidmore Whitelock. "This is to certify," said a sheet of paper and it was a huge map with wide red lines showing air flights between here and Europe.

On my next work day everything seemed

to go purposefully wrong. Because of excavations near the new Senate office building all Constitution Avenue traffic was rerouted and our usual parking place was taken. I was at least fifteen minutes late. As I approached the Annex with my head down against the wind a man on the corner stepped toward me and held out a sheet of paper. Startled I read, "I have cancer of the throat and cannot speak. Please help me." If I stop to talk to him I'll certainly get involved, I reminded myself. New ways of begging every day. My husband continually warns me to beware of such traps. I shook my head.

Inside, ashamed of my calloused behavior, I asked the guard about the man. He had never heard of such a character, he said, certainly not a neighborhood fixture. I went through the narrow central hall. The stuffiness was oppressive. The corridors seemed deserted and my footsteps echoed with a hollow mournful sound. The huge brass doors of the elevators stood in silent rows like entrances to a fort or a prison. No one spoke to me. When the elevator came the woman operator did not greet me but kept on reading her morning paper. The man already on the elevator stared straight ahead and wore a fixed meaningless smile. When he got off on the fourth floor I understood his stare; the fourth floor is where the Braille work is done.

I approached our study room with anxiety. Sure enough, Mr. Whitelock was in the room next to ours, standing at the window. As soon as I hung up my coat he tapped on our door.

"If you can spare the time I'd like to ask
you a few questions," he said settling in a chair
and pulling out a notebook. "This man Schmidt,
Victor R. Schmidt, was a rather busy man, but a
lone wolf, so to speak. No family, no relatives in
this country. Did you at any time notice visitors
or friends stopping in the room to see him?"

"Well, I guess not," I said. "I am in this
room chiefly at the beginning and the end of the
day."

"Have you seen at any time a person of
Arab or Egyptian appearance walking up and
down the corridor outside his room?"

"No, but there are no doubt Arabs and
Egyptians employed here."

"Did he work evenings, do you know?"

"Well, once I stayed late and saw a light in
his room."

"Recently?"

"Oh, let me see. It was the night of the
Open House dinner at the Cosmos Club, three
weeks ago Friday."

He wrote down the date.

"Did he say anything to you at any time to
indicate the state of his health, bad cough or
stomach? The autopsy hasn't come in yet."

I couldn't say. I told Mr. Whitelock that if I
had talked to Mr. Schmidt I would have found
out something, as people always told me things.
He was about to go and then added.

"This man was a quiet uncommunicative
individual. He was in a particular spot, a place
where he could touch opposing sides. Get me?

He may have had more than one iron in the fire.
There is no evidence yet to go on. He learned to
leave no traces. You know, a whole case can
hang upon the most innocent item."

Mr. Whitelock, Mr. Sidmore Whitelock,
gave me his card with a phone number jotted on
it. He told me to call him if I remembered any
piece of evidence that could be used. And all the
time the map was there in the bottom of my
desk drawer.

With this late and inauspicious start
bothering me, I gathered my materials together
and went to the catalogue room to begin work. I
passed through the Reading Room in order to
greet Mr. Burchfield but he was talking to a
helper and did not even give me a nod. I
sharpened a pencil on his desk sharpener, but
he still looked the other way, purposely, it
seemed. Had I infringed on some rule of the
Library? After running into several complica-
tions with numbers and dates of editions in the
main catalogue I decided to go downstairs to the
more complete Official Catalogue. This morning,
as I entered, the door attendant requested my
permit. He never had before. With inconvenience
I got it out of my purse and showed it. He
advised me to be sure to have it renewed before
the expiration date next month. Why should he
ask to see my permit? I had been going in and
out of there for several months. Did he have a
special order to check me?

The cards in the Official Catalogue boxes
or trays are not fastened in by metal rods as are
the others, so one must be very careful in

handling them. Imagine putting them all back in order if once spilled. I was reaching high for "Fitch to Fitzgerald" when a man walked behind me, jogging my arm. I swung the tray down and grabbed it quickly, saving it, thank goodness, but in the process all my sheets of book lists and the manilla folder went on the floor.

"Pardonne," said a man and he turned to help me pick up my papers. He was a square heavy jawed man, skin pox marked (seldom seen today), a character out of Dostoievsky, certainly not the appearance of a scholar. His face got red when he stooped. So did mine, by the way, because he looked at my papers definitely more than he had a right to. This made me a little mad. I'd never seen him there before and I could tell he didn't know his way as he asked questions of an attendant. To make concentrating harder I found myself near a certain little old woman, a file clerk of long time service, who is lame and hard of hearing. She drags a stool with her so she can perch at the high tables.

"How are you feeling today?" one of the other clerks asked her.

"A cold day, very cold day," she replied.

"How is Frances?" much louder this time. "Did Frances get her job?"

"Frances? Oh yes, Frances. Yes, a job, two jobs she has now. I don't understand her. But she is the kind of person who has to have *things*. Things, just things, you know what I mean." And she went on to the"H"'s pulling her stool with her.

Two men leaned across the high table

166

between the cabinets and distracted me with their talk. "This prof. keeps calling me to look up this and that -- this and that -- and I have to pay my good dimes to call him back. My own dimes. What does he think? Am I made of dimes? And if he is a professor he should know this is a Yugoslavian name, not a German name. But -- we have a little place in Virginia, very small of course. We are all the time painting or fixing it. You must come and see us."

The Catalogue and my book list did not tally on the information on four books so I had to go to the stacks and verify my data with the books themselves. This takes a lot of time. Down on Deck 2, the lowest level of the cellar, I began my search. Down there one feels positively crushed by the thought of all the books above. The air seems heavy and sterile as a tomb. Only one other person was down there. I could hear movement in the next aisle. The book I wanted was in the bottom row of the shelf against the wall. They so often seem to be in the bottom row. I wonder why. I reached for it and the lights went out. If this seems melodramatic -- it is, especially when one is far back in the stacks. Turning stack lights out automatically at regular intervals is a way of saving taxpayers' money and I approve of that, of course. The person in the next row started out at the same time as I to turn on the switch and we met at the center.

"Allow me," he said smiling, and pressed the white button.

I went back for my book and he entered

my row, looking at books in the military history section. I checked my book and found it was the first of a series. Two of the group were unfortunately missing. Since I needed all their dates I would have to check elsewhere. The man stayed in my row so long that I finally glanced up at him. I was kneeling to write on my paper on the floor, as one is cramped between those rows. The man was peering at book titles. He was a pale-haired, long-necked individual and he moved his head on his neck for all the world like an animated, dressed-up bookworm out of Walt Disney. He came along the row toward me in sliding undulations, his eyes in heavy glasses popped out like those of a caterpillar as he kept looking at the books. There was no other way out for me. I took off my glasses carefully, gathered together my papers, my purse, and all my quaking reserves of dignity. I walked right up to him and smiled, "Pardon me, may I pass?"

He grunted and stepped back. I waited. I did not care to walk in front of him and gestured that I wished to pass behind. He stepped forward and I slid quickly behind him, and beyond, but not before he had made a deliberate move and our bottoms had bumped hard in the process. When I reached the door of the stack elevator, of course it was not there. With heart pounding I took to the dim hall stairway and came out on Deck 4. I heard the elevator coming up and stepped into it the minute its doors opened. Mr. Caterpillar was there, smiling faintly.

"What floor?" he said, hand poised to press the button.

"Top." I gasped. "R.R. -- reading room."

The elevator went up slowly. It stopped three times and no one else got on. The man was frankly looking at me. I studied my papers and knew real sweat was on my forehead. It occurred to me that I had seen this man before. Was he coming out of the study room next to ours one time last week? Could he be a little *off*? Maybe he was an agent and thought I knew something. When the elevator stopped at the top I felt I had reached heaven. I flew out and around the hall to the Women's Room.

"Nonsense," I said to myself, running cold water over my hands and wiping my face. I looked in the mirror. "At your age he could hardly be a masher and of course he isn't an agent. Only a coincidence." I reached for my purse to get a comb. It wasn't on the chair where I thought I had set it. That man had it. No, a rather frowsy woman in a melon pink coat was going out the door with it.

"Excuse me," I said loudly, "Don't you have my purse?"

She turned back. "Excuse *me*, why do you ask?" Her voice was tragic, a hint of frenzy. Her dark eyes were shadowed by much more than mascarra.

"But it *is* mine."

She opened the purse, then with a quick gesture gave it to me. "So sorry, please believe," she said. "It is exact, *certainement*, like mine."

She opened one of the toilet doors and *certainement*, hanging on a hook was another navy blue purse the same shape as mine. My smile was feeble, but I did smile and shrugged my shoulders in Gallic dismissal. Could someone want my purse for some reason more than money? Maybe it was only my dislike for melon pink coats.

By the middle of the afternoon I began to slow down. I had to go over to the old building to check some books so decided to get some coffee on the way. If you have never been in a long tunnel, that umbilical cord between the Annex and the Main Library, you should go there some time. Like Jonah in the whale you feel like you are washing around inside some monster and you hold your breath pending eruption.

Tremendous fans blow from the middle and ends of the tube and a deafening noise comes out of various rooms full of dynamoes and flickering machines. Two men right behind me were shouting to each other, "When I finish this study I'll apply for a Guggenheim. Someone will appreciate its value," said one. Then the other, "They do not realize I've written four books on this subject already."

At a turn in the corridor I was almost hit by a heavy electric book truck rolling and gaining speed as it came down the slanting tunnel. I jumped aside and grabbed out for support. I found myself leaning on a flimsy railing above the yawning gap of the freight elevator shaft, and as I looked up, the elevator, as big as a room, came down slowly and settled in place with a clanking waddle. For the second time that day I broke out in a sweat. By the time I got to the cafeteria chairs were up on the tables and a rope across the entrance.

"Tough luck," said a woman coming out, "closes at 3:30."

I wondered about my luck. Ever since I found that map things had been going wrong. Was it like the Hope diamond? Was Mr. Schmidt only the first?

In the main reading room of the big library I walked around the circular core desk and off to the stacks through one of the alcoves. I was bound for Deck 42. I entered one of the wobbly cages that serve the old bulding as stack elevators and started up. At Deck 42 it did not stop. I pushed the "down" button, but it kept on going up. The panic of a nightmare I had once right after the war, flashed through my mind. *I dreamed I entered a French bird-cage elevator and the operator refused to take me up. Instead he insisted upon taking me sideways, all over Paris (a Paris in ruins). My children were waiting upstairs. We had only a matter of minutes before the Germans would be there. Still, he refused to take me up.*

Finally, the library elevator stopped and a cheerful attendant got on.

"The trick is to open your door fast when you get to your floor," he advised, "or someone else will take it away from you." I did, and got to my book.

But I decided to walk back down. The open iron stairways and the marble squares of flooring set in steel, gave off a peculiar metallic click as I walked. Decks and decks of books, down and around, down and around I went.

One floor had half-moon windows looking into
the vast central room. I peered through one and
speculated about the people I could see below at
desks and files. Then I saw Mr. Caterpillar. He
was not checking the card file where he was
standing but he was waving his head on his
long neck and staring into my alcove. I went up
again and skirted around until I found a door
out another alcove. I managed to keep out of his
sight and gained the exit hall unnoticed.

Up in our study room I sat down to think.
I really should tell Mr. Whitelock about the map.
I took it out of the drawer and studied it again.
"V. Schmidt," was written in German script in
the right hand corner. That settles it. But what
were all those lines, what did they mean? The
situation in the Near East was critical, that
much I knew. I called Mr. Whitelock from a telephone booth on the second floor.

"Wonderful find!" he said.

" Somehow I had a hunch you would be
able to help. I'm all tied up for the next half
hour. Could you bring the map over here so our
experts could begin on it?"

"Over where?"

"I can't explain, but I'll send a car for you
in twenty minutes."

"I don't ride with strangers," I said, thinking of the admonitions I have often given my
daughter. "How will I know the right car?"

"Hold the wire," he said. Then after a
short wait, "Go to the corner of Second street
and Capitol and wait in front of the Folger
Library, Capitol Street side. In twenty minutes a

black Pontiac will come and stop. The driver will recognize you from what I tell him. By the way, what color is your dress? Navy blue, white collar. You say to the driver, 'Capitol 29'. He will answer, 'Jefferson 66'. Don't be afraid. This is merely precautionary routine. But come immediately with the map. We want to talk to you."

"Can't I know where I am going?"

"For Pete's sake, don't fuss. An important international mission may be at stake. We all must do our part."

Since Mr. Whitelock was right and international missions and the security of our country are daily at stake, I cannot even hint at the details of that ride. Naturally, I did not get beyond the first floor either. Well, at least I gave them the map. That was off my conscience. I could sit back and await a speedy solution.

Mr. Whitelock telephoned me at home the next day and said, "They are working on it. Very significant find. Asia Minor is a vital spot. Oil, you know. And who wants oil? A lot is at stake."

Pipe lines, I muttered to myself. I'll bet those lines were pipc lincs. On whose side was Victor Schmidt?

Last evening I finally brought myself to tell my husband about the map. He was at work in his study and I took him some cocoa before bed time. Like most scholars he likes his notes and books all spread out as he works. He had been reading Xenophon, the Warner edition. I had kept the whole business about Mr. Shcmidt to myself, well, you know how it is. He is always warning me that I'll get into trouble if I go pok-

ing around in other people's business. But I just
had to tell him about this. I even had a copy of
the map which I made quickly, just in case.

My husband studied it carefully. Then he
grabbed one of his books and turned the pages
swiftly. "Just what I thought," and he smiled at
me. "See, it matches exactly."

It did! The map inside the front cover of
the book was almost identical, except for the
writing and numbers on Mr. Schmidt's.

"This is the March of the Ten Thousand,
told in Xenophon's *Anabasie*. Every schoolboy
who has taken Greek knows this story. Don't
you remember how they marched and marched
back and forth, many peraeangs, over Asia
Minor, to India and back?"

"Why would Mr. Schmidt want it?" I
asked.

"Schmidt? Victor R. Schmidt? Why, I
knew him. Sure, he was an investigator, Un-
American Affairs Committee, I believe. But in
reality he was a Greek scholar. Wrote a book
about Greece, in German I believe, before he
came to this country. He spent all his spare
time in the Library trying to complete another.
Worked every night, no family to go home to."

He took the map and held it under his
lamp. "I'll bet these figures are miles. You know
in those days they always spoke of distance in
terms of days of marching, not in miles.
Schmidt has apparently gone over the route,
maybe he himself made it once on some trip and
has figured out the distances on this paper. Too
bad he didn't live to finish his book. He told me

174

he had a heart condition and was working against time. A great loss to scholarship." And he closed his Xenophon tenderly and put it on the shelf.

So I called Mr. Whitelock and told him. It wouldn't have been fair to let them waste any more important time in the investigation. Now you understand why I am happy to be baking a cake. What he said to me I cannot tell you. I am an expert only in cake baking.

"Inga? Thank goodness I caught you home."

"Yah? Inga Olson speaking"

"Inga, this is Mrs. Andersson, Janet Andersson. Remember you cooked that wonderful dinner for us last month -- the celebration for the violinist? Yes, Georgetown, the house with the dining room and kitchen on the lower floor. I know you don't like to work in Georgetown houses, but it isn't to cook that I need you. It's another emergency."

"Yah, I remember. I remember. We had duck with wild rice stuffing. But I am very busy you know. I am booked up weeks in advance."

"But tonight, Inga. Please say, by some stroke of fate, you are free tonight."

"As it happens, Mrs. Andersson, I am free. I am without urgency. I sit in my own kitchen and am right now enjoying my own coffee and a piece of my own cinnamon coffee cake. So what you need? It must be serious or I stay right here."

"Inga, have you read in the *Washington Post* about the coming visit of the Swedish novelist, Solvig Holm? Well, never mind, she is here, right in my third floor guest room. Yes, and not at all happy. She is sick. Definitely. Vomiting up every twenty minutes. And here am I, giving a reception for her at eight o'clock this very evening!"

"So -- a Swedish writer? It is the Washington water, Mrs. Andersson. My father-in-law, every time he comes to town his stomach . . ."

"Water or no, she is in no shape to stand in a receiving line tonight. Fifty to seventy people will be here, the Pen Women, my AAUW friends, the Writers' Club, the Literary Society, even the English professors at Mr. Andersson's college. Inga, it is dreadful!"

"Poor thing. Have you given her some soda water, or tea?"

"Nothing stays down. The doctor will be here soon. But oh, Inga, this is what I want you to do. Do you know you are the image of Solvig, even to her braids? Come, stand in line and be Solvig. You speak some Swedish. You won't have to say more than 'How do you do'. If you need to say more, Mr. Andersson will stay right beside you. He speaks Swedish and can pretend to translate for you."

"So -- you want me to be a writer. She looks like me? Yah, now that would be good, now wouldn't it? Inga, Inga the cook. Of course I am a special cook. I get fifty dollars for a dinner and am worth every cent. Did you read the menu of the dinner at the White House they gave that poor visiting prime minister last night? No wonder our politicals have ulcers -- such fancy stuff!"

"The White House gives famous dinners, Inga, especially now with the French chef. But that's not the point, Inga. Will you come?"

"Could I wear a black velvet cape, maybe some big rings, and perhaps some eye shadow?"

"Heavens no. You're thinking of Edith Sitwell, or Isak Dineson. Solvig Holm is natural, in apearance I mean. No, above all, no eye shadow."

"Oh, I'm so sorry. Maybe a long velvet dress then, and some pearls, real ones? I have never worn real pearls, Mrs. Andersson, never in my life."

"You can probably wear one of Solvig's dresses. You'll have to talk to her somehow between her trips to the bathroom. You can wear my pearls, Inga, anything, if you'll come. After all my plans and all the publicity -- she's in town only this weekend, and if I am not able to produce her for all my friends . . .!"

"Sure, I know, Mrs. Andersson. But what if they ask me about my books. Then what do I say? I have never read a book by Solvig Holm. Tell me, is she a good writer? She must be a good writer. I do not wish to stand up in the place of a bad writer."

"Don't worry, Inga. If anyone asks you, say you do not speak enough English to explain so difficult a subject. Let me see, her last novel was *The Wedding Ring*, the one before that, *Princess Feather*. Her book, *Hit and Miss* had bad reviews in England but good ones here. None of the others have been translated."

"What kind of writer am I -- good or bad? You do not answer me."

"Good or bad? It's not that simple. Her

stories are symbolic. They tend toward the mysterious. You've seen a Bergman movie? Yes, a bit like them, heavy with meaning and not always clear."

"I do not like Mr. Bergman's movies. I have seen two. They are all about early times, sin and unhappy people."

"Now Inga, you won't have to defend your writing. Nobody will want to discuss it. All you need to do is stand there and smile and shake hands and keep your mouth shut. No, low heels will be all right. Of course you will be symbolic, if you look at it that way, but that's not the point right now."

"Will I maybe be good enough to someday get the Nobel Prize?"

"How do I know? Seriously, I doubt it. Who can say? I wouldn't put anything past Solvig, even the Nobel Prize. She has got almost everything she ever wanted. She has lived all over the world, has had three husbands, a son, decorations, denunciations. Oh, and to think she is here, in my house, and . . . she is Mr. Andersson's second cousin, by the way. That is why she is visiting us."

"Well, if I am full of symbols and strange stories and will never get the Prize, I don't know."

"Oh Inga, don't back out. You can always say to people, 'Washington is a beautiful city'. That will start them off. You won't have to say another thing. No one will listen anyway. You know how it is at big parties -- everyone talking loudly and at once. It is even worse with women writers, they'll want to tell you about their latest story. And if anyone from the press is there . . . Oh, my God, they might take pictures! Well, if you see anyone aiming a camera at you, turn your head so they'll get your braids. We'll wrap them around exactly like Solvig's. No, I won't forget about the pearls. Yes, they are real, not fakes, not symbols."

"Will you have champagne, Mrs. Andersson, surely for such a famous person -- and maybe a souffle for the buffet?"

"Forget about the food this time. The caterer is taking care of everything. Yes, champagne. We'll serve in the dining room downstairs and also set up a bar in the library. If you wish I'll pay you your regular fee of fifty dollars, but under the circumstances . . ."

"No, no fee. But I am thinking of something I would like, Mrs. Andersson."

"What is it? If at all possible . . ."

"I think that I would like one of Solvig's books. Yes, that is what I would like. And on the front page I want it to say, 'to Inga Olson from Solvig Holm.' "

"That'll be quite easy. Now, can you come about seven? We must allow time to get you into a long dress. No, no eye shadow. Yes, I won't forget the pearls. Goodbye, you'll never know how grateful . . ."

"Yah, I come. And if they ask for my picture I turn my head just as they press the button. We will fool them, Mrs. Andersson. They will see Solvig, the great Swedish writer, ha! ha!"

¥

"Oh, Mrs. Farnham, how good of you to come. Yes, it is a bit foggy tonight. Did you find a place to park? If I can get Mrs. Holm's attention, I want her to meet you. I've told her about the Literary Society, one of the oldest in Washington. Solvig, this is Mrs. Farnham, president this year of our Washington Literary Society. You have heard me speak of her."

Inga, regal in burgundy velvet and a string of matched pearls, held out her hand graciously, "How do you do, Mrs. Farnham."

"We have been anticipating this evening for weeks," Mrs. Farnham said emphatically. She wore a black lace stole over a black all-purpose, all-occasion, all-season dress. "In fact, I went down to the Library of Congress this week and could only find two of your novels to read."

"Only three have been translated," Mr. Andersson said quickly. His tall stooped figure loomed up above all the women. "Her first one, *Roman Stripe* I believe, was written in Italian, as you may know. Most of her writings since the war . . ."

"How marvelous! Yes, I know. I try to keep up, but the new books come out so fast. Did you see the review of Steinbeck's book last Sunday? They really missed his point, don't you think? Oh, excuse me," as she bumped against another woman at her elbow. "Oh, it's Mrs. Buckingham from Bethesda, how nice to see you. Have you met the authoress yet? Isn't she elegant? Yes, perfect simplicity. So perfect in fact it almost seems unnatural."

With a glass in one hand and an un-lighted cigarette in the other Mrs. Buckingham eyed the famous one with a squint, "Yes, I've met her. Do you think it is true -- about her during the war? Her husband disappeared so mysteriously. Some say he was pro-German."

Inga leaned toward Mr. Andersson and whispered. Mr. Andersson nodded and then turned to Mrs. Buckingham.

"Allow me," he produced a lighter for her cigarette. "I couldn't help overhearing. Solvig tells me Mr. Holm was a member of a peace mission, you may remember. Too bad it didn't succeed. The war might have ended sooner."

Mrs. Andersson looked at her husband in amazement, "Where did you hear that?"

"Of course," Inga said proudly, "My hus-band could not explain such things in those days. He was a good man."

Two young and vivacious women came up, young enough to be frontier-minded and too young to remember the frontier. Janet Anders-son took the hand of the first, a blonde with her hair in a French topknot, "This is Marian Martin, Mrs. Holm, our publicity chairman. She also writes children's books."

Inga held the blonde's hand, "Children's books," she repeated with a heavy Swedish accent.

"Only one, so far," the blonde smiled depreciatingly, "Nothing as intellectual or as complicated as yours, Mrs. Holm."

"Washington is a beautiful city," Inga said slowly.

Marian Martin seemed puzzled, then she smiled broadly, "Mrs. Holm, you can't fool me. I read your books. They are wise and full of double meanings. Tell me, in *The Wedding Ring*, didn't you intend the ring to mean not only the gold band she wore but the whole family circle she married into, a circle she could not escape?"

Inga shook her head sadly and put her hand on the pearls, "All things have many meanings." She turned to Mr. Andersson, "Explain. A ring is a ring."

Mr. Andersson sighed and fumbled in his pocket for his pipe and then began to fill it meticulously from his leather tobacco pouch. His lean nordic face was impassive in the flash of his light, "You are aware, Mrs. Martin, that symbolism in light doses is necessary, yes, is basically essential for all thought. We cannot speak without abstractions, without generalities. The more philosophical or poetic the writer the more he is likely to succumb to the use of symbols. However, Hemingway, for instance . . ."

Marian Martin started, "Hemingway . . .," then moved politely aside to let her friend have her place.

"Elizabeth Harrington," said Mrs. Andersson, introducing a tall angular person whose fashionable silk shift gave somehow the impression of a tweed suit and walkers.

The woman shook Inga's hand vigorously, "This is such a pleasure to meet an internationally famous writer. It is strange, Mrs. Holm, but I feel I know you very well after reading your books, even better than Janet here. Though we are old friends, aren't we Janet? How many years?"

"Elizabeth has completed a novel, Solvig. She is already on the second revision. A great accomplishment!" and Janet Andersson patted her friend's hand.

"Tosh, it just takes perseverance, and then a publisher, of course. But right now I am completely stumped on the title. How have you been so fortunate in your titles, Mrs. Holm? They are absolutely perfect. You must have a sixth sense, an ear for such things. But with your mystical perception you probably . . ."

"Quilt patterns," Inga said solemnly.

"Yes?" Both the Anderssons leaned toward her, on guard.

"Quilt patterns, you know -- quilts. I name my books after them."

There was complete silence. Elizabeth was the first to recover. "How delightful! I must tell Jerry. He will simply not believe me. But it is true, now that I go over them. How very clever, and also so very symbolic! Don't you think so, Janet?"

Janet Andersson was slow to respond, "Symbolic? Symbolic? Oh yes, of course, I see what you mean. Henry James said something in the *Art of the Novel* about writing being like the weaving of threads of many colors into patterns on a giant tapestry. The possibilities of choice are tremendous. Solvig chooses quilts, not tapestry, for her patterns."

"So Scandinavian too," Elizabeth Harrington beamed. "Such a homey comforting symbol, covering so much. Incredible!"

Mr. Andersson nodded emphatically, "Don't be surprised at us Swedes." He bowed in Inga's direction.

"My mother had many quilts. I honor her memory." Inga looked like a Kirstin Flagstad about to render the "Ride of the Valkyries."

Janet Andersson muttered to her husband, "Wasn't Solvig about fourteen when her mother died? There was some story of the mother separating from her Swede when Solvig was little. Took her off to Rome. The Italian interlude hardly called for many quilts."

She turned with a quick smile to a fragile elderly woman, "Dear Mrs. Charing, I am so glad you were able to get out for our party. How are you tonight? And Dr. Charing? I hope he is well."

The little woman came close to Janet Andersson and whispered, "I am not very strong but I had to come to see the novelist. Since he retired, you know, I can't get Charles to go to these things. But I go. Washington is a wonderful city, so much to do, never dull, never for a minute." She swayed slightly and pressed her hand hard on her hostess's arm for support.

"And the dear sweet thing! Isn't she a beauty, so refreshing, such talent. I remember when we did our hair like that. I remember the wonderful parties the Blisses used to give at Dumbarton Oaks, before they moved. Such a place for a party, and with music too. But we don't have time these days to entertain in the grand manner. Rush -- rush -- ugly cars everywhere -- so many people. I wish, my dear, you could have known Washington when it *was* beautiful."

"Mrs. Holm," Janet Andersson said, "This is a very special person, one of the founders of our Writer's Club, Mrs. Charing. She had been its guiding spirit. I don't know what we would do without her."

"My dear," Mrs. Charing said, peering closely at Inga, "You are a joy to behold. A real live author! Not many of us publish you know, but we write -- we write." She laughed as she looked around the crowded room. "Pardon me if I confess I have not read any of your books, Mrs. Holm. I have given up reading the new things and am just rereading the old ones, the ones I know I like -- Shakespeare and the Greeks and . . . Now after seeing you I may get one of your books. Maybe Charles and I can read it aloud to each other. We do that, you know. Saves eyes, and it's unbelievable pleasure. Which one of your novels would you recommend for reading aloud?"

"Reading aloud," Inga repeated. She looked at Mr. Andersson, but he wore a slightly amused expression and was volunteering nothing.

"Washington is . . .," she began, hesitated, then said formly, "Stay with Shakespeare."

Mrs. Charing clapped her hands and her little beaded evening bag rattled, "Delightful -- I knew it! What other author would be as sensible, as depreciating of her own works, as generous as you! I love you, Solvig Holm. Now I am determined to read you. Charles will be enchanted when I tell him."

"May I get you some champagne, Solvig?" Mr. Andersson bowed in a courtly fashion.

Mrs. Andersson frowned at her husband. He smiled as if he were happy about something.

"No, thank you," Inga said. "I do not care for drinking. It is not good for my -- for my symbolism."

"You are absolutely right, Mrs. Holm," said Mrs. Charing, turning back on her way toward the door. "I wish more modern authors felt as you do about drinking. Perhaps they would write something besides trash. Bilge, trash, drugs, what have you! Look at Tennessee Williams!"

"Tennessee's Williams," Inga repeated.

"I see you agree with me," Mrs. Charing beamed. "I am so pleased. A beautiful party, Janet, my dear. Yes, I've been downstairs. Your dining room is perfect, absolutely perfect, as always. Too bad the Swedish Ambassador did not come. Oh, in Stockholm. Well, my dear, see you at our next meeting. Don't forget, Thursday. Goodbye. And goodbye, dear wonderful Solvig Holm. Keep on writing, keep on writing. We need good clean writers like you. How this world needs them!"

Janet Andersson beckoned to a young woman who had been hovering in the background. "This is our poet," she said. "Betty Miles, don't hide. She writes verses on shopping bags and children's coloring books. Some day she will collect them and publish, but now, I would say with Mrs. Charing, 'just keep writing'. "

Inga held out her hand to the small woman in a nun-like suit and neat white collar, "Keep writing," she repeated.

Betty Miles sighed, "Why? I often ask myself. But do you know, last night at three a.m. with the baby, I thought a brand new thought. You have no idea how much it helped."

"She has six children," Janet Andersson explained.

"Six children," Inga beamed in admiration. "I had only one. Six -- that is good. Yah, very good."

"Oh, thank you, Mrs. Holm," the young face lighted under Inga's benevolent gaze. "You have no idea how much you help me. I get discouraged easily, yet, to know someone understands and believes in one. It is wonderful! It isn't easy, is it? Writing is really hard work."

"Hard work," Inga shrugged, "But if you love what you do . . ."

"And you still love what you are doing?" Betty Miles asked hopefully. "After all the publicity, your fights with publishers, and some of

the dreadful reviews jealous critics write, you
still say it is worth while? I am so happy. It gives
us courage to keep at it, doesn't it, Mrs. Andersson?"

Janet Andersson smiled at Betty Miles
fondly as she moved away into the crowd, then
turned to her husband, "Didn't I hear Solvig say
at lunch that she would never pick up the pen
again, that her publisher was a jail keeper, that
all critics were vultures. Probably because they
dug up a story about her winter in Majorca. A
London paper, I believe, called it a Balearic Idyll!
A young man young enough to be her son . . .!"

"My son died during the war," Inga
announced gravely. "Helping the Danish people
in their underground."

"Are you speaking as Inga or Solvig?"
asked Mr. Andersson in a serious tone.

"Both are gone," said Inga. She pulled
herself back and closed her eyes, removing herself completely. Mr. Andersson relit his pipe.
Janet Andersson slipped her foot out of one
silver pump for a blissful half minute, then
straightened up quickly.

"Geraldine, from the paper, is coming this
way," she nudged Inga. "Be careful, the press."

"Would you care to make a statement,
Mrs. Holm?" asked the intense young reporter in
sleeveless black velvet, the dress uniform of the
feminine press. "What is your opinion of our
American women novelists today?"

"Good, good," Inga nodded and looked
over to Mr. Andersson who nodded back.

"I see. So you feel our American women writers, Katherine Ann Porter, Pearl Buck, Lillian Smith, Carson McCullers, to mention a few, express the American scene in all its variety, and are able to meet the men in ability and sensitivity?" Inga kept on nodding. "I am so glad to hear you say that." She took out a small notebook. "And Mr. Steinbeck, our Nobel Prize winner, how do you rate him with Faulkner, or with Hemingway?"

"Steinbeck, Mr. Steinbeck," Inga hesitated and Mr. Andersson cleared his throat. But she went on, "Mr. Steinbeck is still alive, I guess . . "

"Oh, I see, you place him above all the others. Not everyone would agree with you, Mrs. Holm. Personally I feel he has not been fully appreciated in this country. But people will understand why a writer of your type would prefer him to the blood and sex of Hemingway and the southern decadence of Faulkner. And now about your own works, of your total body of works, let me see, ten novels and two biographies I believe, which one is your favorite?"

"So many?" Inga looked surprised. She sighed heavily, "Ten! Well, I like best the next one. Always the next one."

"Oh, Mrs. Holm, you will not play favorites I can see. But what is your next one to be called? Does it have a title yet?"

Inga reflected. Then a great smile broke over her face and she chuckled, "Maybe I call it *Crazy Quilt, may* be." She laughed with contagious abandon.

"This is great. I can hardly wait to get this out. Thank you so much for your gracious co-operation. It has been a great pleasure to inter-view you. And now, Bill wants to take some pictures. Yes, for the paper tomorrow. Bill, a shot of the three together, don't you think, right there in front of those dark curtains, excellent. Oh, Mrs. Holm, you moved. So sorry. We'll have to take another. Perhaps this one . . ."

¥

After the last goodbyes the trio sank into deep chairs by the fireplace. "My feet!" moaned Janet Andersson. Mr. Andersson loosened his tie and unbottoned his vest. Inga sat rather pre-cisely, her feet on the floor, her gaze dreamily on the fire which now was a glow of embers. A maid came in and began to gather glasses onto a tray.

"Lu, be a dear and bring us up a bite on a tray," begged Janet. "Biscuits and ham. Any left? How about some liver paté? I am starved."

Mr. Andersson rose, "Surely champagne is now in order. I wish to drink to Solvig, not only the one we hope is fast asleep upstairs, but to Solvig present." He saluted Inga.

"Inga," said Janet Andersson, going over to a reading table and coming back with a book and a pen. "Here -- Solvig's *The Wedding Ring*. I wish you would autograph it for us."

Inga studied the photograph on the back jacket of the volume, Then in a dignified manner, opened to the flyleaf and wrote, "To my friends, Mr. and Mrs. Andersson. Pearls and no eye sha-dow. Solvig."

191

Epilogue

By the Sea . . . Newport, August 1994

They were taking the sea drive on a Sunday afternoon. Three generations -- the daughter driving, her mother (the grandmother) beside her. In the back seat two granddaughters -- college girls, one red headed, one blonde, the whole car redolent with their beauty.

"The 'Breakers'," pointed out the daughter, "A line of tourists already waiting to get in."

"I see," said the grandmother. "Mr. Vanderbilt's fortress from sea and time. Certainly sturdy."

"I always like this view," said the daughter as she stopped at a lookout.

Disturbed sea gulls screeched overhead, waves crept up to the rocks and fell back, fell back.

"Tide is coming in," called the girls as they flew down the steps to explore the rocks below.

The daughter leaned on the balustrade and gazed toward the gray blue horizon. "Ships out there", she remarked.

A young couple, carrying their toddler in his stroller up the steps, smiled at their little son as they set him down, then smiled at each other as they moved on.

The water washed over the rocks, then fell back, fell back.

A car pulled in behind them, music blaring.

The grandmother winced, then listened. The
man in the car got out, leaned on his car door
with eyes on the water, transfixed by the music.
The song poured out confidently, sure, almost
defiantly, incredibly beautiful, maybe a Verdi.

The song ended, the man got into his car
and drove away. The daughter signaled to the
girls to come in. They ran up the stairs panting,
laughing, and flopped into their seats.

"Wait! Stop!" the grandmother cried from
the innermost depths of her being.

But the sea gulls dropped to the water,
then soared up again, cutting their patterns in
the sky.

The daughter held open the car door for
her mother to enter.

And the waves splashed hard against the
rocks, then fell back.

Splashed hard against the rocks, then fell
back, splashed, fell back, fell back.

*A simple allegory
about the
relentlessness
of time.*

CLS